THE
MARRIAGE MENDER

A Couple's Guide for Staying Together

Thomas A. Whiteman, Ph.D. & Thomas G. Bartlett, Ph.D.
WITH RANDY PETERSEN

NAVPRESS

BRINGING TRUTH TO LIFE
NavPress Publishing Group
P.O. Box 35001, Colorado Springs, Colorado 80935

The Navigators is an international Christian organization. Our mission is to reach, disciple, and equip people to know Christ and to make Him known through successive generations. We envision multitudes of diverse people in the United States and every other nation who have a passionate love for Christ, live a lifestyle of sharing Christ's love, and multiply spiritual laborers among those without Christ.

NavPress is the publishing ministry of The Navigators. NavPress publications help believers learn biblical truth and apply what they learn to their lives and ministries. Our mission is to stimulate spiritual formation among our readers.

Library of Congress Catalog Card Number: 96-10991
ISBN 08910-99255

Cover illustration: Larry Martin/Scott Hull & Associates

This publication is designed to provide accurate and authoritative information in regard to the subject matter covered. It is sold with the understanding that the author and the publisher are not engaged in rendering legal, accounting, or other professional service. If legal advice or other expert assistance is required, the services of a competent professional person should be sought. *From a Declaration of Principles jointly adopted by a Committee of the American Bar Association and a Committee of Publishers.*

Unless otherwise identified, all Scripture quotations in this publication are taken from the *HOLY BIBLE: NEW INTERNATIONAL VERSION* ® (NIV®). Copyright © 1973, 1978, 1984 by International Bible Society. Used by permission of Zondervan Publishing House. All rights reserved. Another version used is the *New American Standard Bible* (NASB), © The Lockman Foundation 1960, 1962, 1963, 1968, 1971, 1972, 1973, 1975, 1977.

Whiteman, Tom.
    The marriage mender : a couple's guide for staying together / Thomas A.
Whiteman and Thomas G. Bartlett.
        p.   cm.
    ISBN 0-89109-925-5 (paper)
    1. Marriage.   2. Marriage counseling.   I. Bartlett, Thomas, 1954- .
II. Title.
HQ734.W573   1996
306.81—dc20   96-10991
                                                                        CIP

Printed in the United States of America

1 2 3 4 5 6 7 8 9 10 11 12 13 14 15 / 00 99 98 97 96

FOR A FREE CATALOG OF
NAVPRESS BOOKS & BIBLE STUDIES,
CALL 1-800-366-7788 (USA)
or 1-416-499-4615 (CANADA)

▼ ▼

Contents

To my parents . . .

> Thank you for your loving marriage—
> an invaluable gift to your children.

To my wife, Jemmie . . .

> Thank you for the encouragement and inspiration for
> this book. I look forward to spending the rest of our lives
> together. I love you.
>
> —Tom Bartlett

▼　▼　▼

To my wife, Lori . . .

> Thank you for your support of my ministry—the many
> weekends away, the hectic schedule, and for staying
> behind to care for our children. You have been the wind
> beneath my wings! Thanks too for my trip to Alaska.
>
> —Tom Whiteman

▼ ▼

Looking to the Future, Not the Past: An Introduction

When was the last time you had a fight with your spouse? Either a shouting match or a slow burner. Last month? Last week? This morning? Is there a lot of tension in your marriage? Welcome to the human race.

How did you resolve your fight? Did one or both of you compromise? Did you apologize? Did you kiss and make up? Or did you agree to disagree?

"I know I need to love my wife," a man said to his counselor, "but can you help me *live with her?*" The fact is, he knows how to live with his wife. He does it every day. What he wants is a way to make it easier, a way to make it better. He is not finding fulfillment in his marriage, and he desperately wants to. Maybe you can relate.

You picked up this book because you're fighting a lot—or simmering, or just glaring. You don't like the way things are in your marriage and you want to make things better. The good news is that you *can.* With God's help, you and your spouse have the power to make a real partnership out of something that's now just a coexistence.

There's more good news: You're not alone. Many couples panic when they feel the initial flush of romance fading. They're not *in love* anymore, and so they fear the whole relationship is over.

Our culture teaches that there is one *right person,* who will make your marriage an eternally happy and romantic experience, who will magically meet all your needs. But once the honeymoon is over, you thud back to reality. When conflict arises, you begin to question whether you married the right person. Questioning the validity of the marriage, letting your dissatisfaction steep, eventually the search begins again for the right person. The ideal of the perfect mate is like the Holy Grail—the expectations are impossibly high and exceptionally strong. Even when people realize (mentally) that the quest is potentially damaging, they continue to seek the ideal lover.

Few people enter into marriage with plans to split up after a few years. Most picture a life-long, love-filled relationship, characterized by sharing, intimacy, and safety. But when we feel that our dream is dying, it hurts. Our hopes of fulfillment are dashed. We suddenly see all the warts and woes of our once-perfect spouses, and we blame them for not making us happy.

As counselors, we hear this desperation all the time:

"What can I do? He won't change."

"She says she just doesn't love me anymore."

"No one seems to care about *my* needs."

The inflated expectations make the problem worse than it is, but the problem remains. We want to be happy in marriage, and we're not. What can we do?

SEEKING A SOLUTION

There's an exciting new trend in marriage counseling today. Once therapists tended to promote personal fulfillment above all, recommending divorce if a marriage got in the way of individual growth. But now more and more therapists and researchers are seeing the value of keeping couples together. This "revolutionary" idea is, of course, not new at all to Christian counselors. It's just exciting to see the secular counseling community embracing these same ideals.[1]

In addition, there is a growing body of new research, techniques, and materials designed to help troubled couples resolve problems so that they can stay together. One such study was able to predict with 94 percent accuracy which couples would stay married and then identified the most important ingredients in their successes.[2]

We have found these techniques effective in our workshops and work with couples. Many deeply troubled marriages are now showing remarkable improvement, and in a relatively short time. This book tells many of their stories. We hope that your marriage, whether it is deeply troubled or just in need of some fine tuning, will become another one of these success stories. (And that you will share that success with us, so that we can include you in our next edition.)

WHY ANOTHER MARRIAGE BOOK?

Many marriage manuals, particularly Christian ones, extol the importance of love, commitment, and submission to God and one another. We believe in these foundational truths, but we've noticed that Christians, even though they have heard these truths, are still divorcing at about the same rate as nonChristians (nearly 50 percent). More help is needed! Couples are asking us for *practical* help in dealing with their day to day squabbles. They want *workable* ideas for increasing the level of intimacy in their marriages.

That is what this book is designed to provide!

A UNIQUE APPROACH

- ▼ Practical
- ▼ Realistic
- ▼ Solution-based
- ▼ Safe

The Marriage Mender will give you the tools to make positive and fulfilling changes in your marriage. It's full of proven principles and techniques, which you can apply immediately to begin fixing problems, improving communication, and making your marriage last.

While our guidelines are based on biblical principles, we take a *practical* approach, emphasizing specific steps that you can implement in order to improve your marriage. These action steps will be woven throughout the book, with activities for couples or small groups included at the end of each chapter. You can decide whether you want to write in this book or keep a separate journal.

Marriage is hard work—no doubt about it. When you think about the vast differences a man and a woman bring to a marriage, it becomes clear why there is work involved.

- ▼ God has given us decidedly different wiring—physically, emotionally, and socially. Whether we attribute the differences to biology, social conditioning, or both, they make a big difference in how we think and act.
- ▼ Each of us is a product of the very specific culture of our family of origin, affecting the way we view relationships or even how the toothpaste tube should be squeezed.
- ▼ And of course we each have individual distinctions—intelligence, personality traits, interests, and hobbies.

In light of our differences, how can marriage *not* be characterized by some struggle and work? Recognizing that no relationship is ever perfect, we take a *realistic* approach in this book, giving you true-to-life examples to help you have more realistic expectations about your own relationship.

We've also integrated some of the most recent and successful techniques being used by marriage and family therapists. Even though this book is not intended to be a substitute for counseling, we have included some of the exercises and methods that we actually employ in counseling sessions. Many of these techniques are based on an exciting new trend in counseling called solution-based therapy. In our *solution-based* approach, we focus on the future of the relationship, rather than on past battles. What can you do to create a better tomorrow? We will explain this new treatment and apply it to our marriage-building skills.

We also believe in the *safe* approach. In an atmosphere of

safety, both partners feel secure enough to share their gut-level thoughts and feelings. We will provide tools for you and your spouse to begin creating an emotionally safe environment in your home, conducive to change, growth, and intimacy.

ABOUT US

Both authors are Christian psychologists who work with a lot of troubled couples. Tom Bartlett practices with Behavioral Health-care Consultants in Lancaster, Pennsylvania, while Tom Whiteman is the president of Life Counseling Services in Paoli, Pennsylvania. We have conducted seminars on marriage, and have also done considerable work in the area of divorce recovery through Fresh Start Seminars. Our work with separated and divorced individuals, as well as their children, has inspired much of the motivation to provide this book to people who want to make their marriages work. We are convinced that saving a marriage is preferable to picking up the pieces after a divorce.

In our counseling practices we have seen dozens of couples, on the brink of divorce, turn their relationships around. We take great joy in knowing many who have used the principles presented in this book to create happy, healthy marriages. We believe there is hope and help for *your* marriage, too!

As you read, you should know that some of the anecdotal illustrations in this book are true to life and are included with the permission of the persons involved. All other illustrations are composites of real situations, and any resemblance to people living or dead is coincidental.

▼　▼　▼

If you would like to sponsor a marriage-building seminar or to get other helpful materials, write Fresh Start Seminars, 63 Chestnut Road, Paoli, PA 19301, or call (800)882-2799.

▼　▼　▼

Randy Petersen is a freelance writer who resides in Westville, New Jersey.

PART ONE

▼

The Agony that Leads to Safety and Solutions

▼ ▼

CHAPTER ONE

Unmasking Marital Myths

Having unrealistic expectations about marriage is high on the list of things that destroy otherwise reasonably sound relationships.[1]

You're walking along the beach with your spouse, hand in hand, the waves lapping at your feet. The love of your life turns to you and says, "Honey, if I were terribly maimed, or perhaps paralyzed in an automobile accident, would you still love me? Would you still stay with me and take care of me?"

Gulp. What do you say? "Yes, I guess. But why did you have to bring that up *now?*"

The essence of the question is this: Do you really love me unconditionally? And will you still love me no matter how I look or how I perform?

The *right* answer is, of course, "I'll always love you, dear — no matter what happens"! If you don't give the right answer, or even if you hesitate a bit too long, your romantic moment is lost forever and you are consigned to the doghouse.

If that question comes up during your honeymoon, it's fairly easy to give the right answer. Your relationship is fresh and wonderful. What could possibly change this exquisite feeling?

But two years, four years, maybe even ten years into your marriage, you look back and wonder what happened to that kind of love. You're not maimed or paralyzed, yet you have to work for any kind of attention in the relationship. Sometimes you may even feel unwelcome in your own home.

SO WHAT WENT WRONG?

What happened? What went wrong with your love? Nothing.

That might surprise you. Nothing went wrong? But it was all so certain and true and unconditional back then! Now it's strained and tense. Obviously *something* happened!

What you experienced was the normal evolution of a relationship. Reality set in. You progressed from the normal infatuation stage of your relationship —with the utter certainty of unconditional love—into the negotiation stage. This stage may be just as loving, but it's less blind. Instead of protesting quickly and loudly that we will always be at the side of our maimed mates, once we're in the negotiation stage we tend to consider the realities of the pain and sacrifice involved. (You'll find more about this in the next chapter.)

*The expectation that marital love will always be exciting, romantic, and unconditional is just one of many **marriage myths** that abound in our culture.*

The problem is with our expectations. The newlywed who asks the question about being paralyzed in an accident is looking for confirmation that this feeling of infatuation will last a lifetime. It won't.

The expectation that marital love will always be exciting, romantic, and unconditional is just one of many marriage myths that abound in our culture. Think about it: Where do we learn about marriage and love? From our *parents*, certainly (if we were raised in a double-parent home). But also from *TV, movies,* and *music.* We have studied marriage in the homes of Ozzie and Harriet, the Brady Bunch, and the Huxtable family. We have learned the language of love from crooners and rappers. No wonder we have unrealistic expectations! Some people also learn about marriage from *religion,* in preaching, Sunday school classes, or seminars.

Both of us have seen many marriages that could have been good marriages, except for the spouses' strong belief in a marital myth. What a couple believes a marriage *should* look like can drastically taint the way they view their relationship and their lives.

MYTH CHECK

KEY
1. "I strongly disagree."
2. "I don't think so."
3. "I'm neutral/I don't know."
4. "I think it's true."
5. "I strongly agree."

1. God has created one right person for me to marry. If I stay in God's will and marry that person, I will have the best chance at a successful marriage.

      1   2   3   4   5

2. People who are madly in love from the beginning of their relationship are more likely to stay together in marriage.

      1   2   3   4   5

3. Loving relationships grow stronger and stronger throughout life.

      1   2   3   4   5

4. Happy couples have fewer arguments than unhappy couples.

      1   2   3   4   5

5. If my spouse refuses to work on the relationship, there is very little I can do to change things.

      1   2   3   4   5

(continued on page 18)

(continued from page 17)

6. If I am happily married, I will not fantasize about another person.

   1   2   3   4   5

7. Happily married couples share many of the same activities and interests.

   1   2   3   4   5

8. Having a strong faith is a good way to avoid temptation in my relationship.

   1   2   3   4   5

9. Happy couples are more likely to pray and read the Bible together.

   1   2   3   4   5

10. A lack of passion in my marriage is a sign that the relationship is in trouble.

   1   2   3   4   5

SCORING

While this is not a scientific study, it will help you think about your attitudes and your expectations about marriage. Just as a guideline, consider the following scoring interpretation:

▼ If you scored between 40 and 50, you may have a very idealized view of marriage.

▼ If you scored between 20 and 39, you probably have a fairly realistic view of marriage.

▼ If you scored between 10 and 19, then you may be realistic, but you must also watch out for the possibility that you have become somewhat cynical about marriage.

MYTH ONE: A CHRISTIAN MARRIAGE IS IMMUNE TO MAJOR CONFLICT

Perpetrators of the myth:

▼ Christian tendency to cover up problems
▼ Naiveté about difficulties in the Christian life

As I* conduct Fresh Start divorce recovery seminars around the country, I often hear divorced people say something like this: "My marriage didn't work out because I made the mistake of marrying a nonChristian. The next time will be different because I'll marry a Christian."

I agree that Christians should marry Christians. But this does not guarantee any special protection from marital problems. The research indicates that Christians divorce at about the same rate as nonChristians. There may be some differences within certain denominations or within specific groups, but overall we don't seem to have any kind of *secret formula* that keeps us together.

According to the research, the differences lie in the reasons we give for divorcing. NonChristians are more likely to indicate incompatibility as the reason for divorce, while Christians seem to hang in there until things get much worse. The top reasons Christians give for divorce are adultery, substance abuse, physical or verbal abuse, and abandonment.[2]

My counseling experience leads me to conclude that Christians, or at least people who call themselves Christians, are just as capable as nonChristians of committing even the most heinous offenses. There's a bumper sticker that reads: "Christians aren't perfect, just forgiven." Amen to that. I believe that those who truly seek a close relationship with Christ experience the sanctifying work of His Spirit, but there are still struggles. Our spirits may be willing, but our flesh is weak. And our weakness has serious effects on those closest to us—including our husbands and wives.

*All first person pronouns in this chapter refer to Tom Whiteman.

So it would be wrong and even dangerous to assume that our Christianity immunizes us from marital conflict or even divorce. When we assume that we are not susceptible to problems, we let down our guard and become *more* susceptible. We need to acknowledge our vulnerability and determine to do the right thing, knowing that it is only the grace of God and the work of the Holy Spirit that make us any different from the nonbeliever.

Unfortunately, many Christian couples are reluctant to admit to themselves that they're having problems because "that would be unspiritual." They're even less likely to seek help from their pastors or Christian counselors. Marital conflict is a private matter, to be sure, but we make things worse with a judgmental attitude. How often have you heard a request brought up in a prayer meeting, "Let's pray for John and Betty. Their marriage is in trouble"? If you have, it may have been in a spirit of gossip or judgment. But at a time like this John and Betty sorely need the church's love and support.

Christians need help just like everyone else. Christian husbands and wives can have incompatible personalities, fight unfairly, have frustrations based in poor communication, and even have affairs. So what's the difference? Christians have the model of Christ, who humbled Himself, who put others before Himself. Christians have received God's forgiveness, and we know we need to forgive others. Christians have the power of the Holy Spirit, though we don't always tap into it.

It makes no sense to perpetuate the myth that Christians always have close marriages, which only leads to false security, naiveté, and hypocrisy. Let's own up to our problems and ask for God's help in dealing with them.

MYTH TWO: MARRIAGE PARTNERS SHOULD AGREE ON MOST THINGS

Perpetrators of the myth:

- ▼ "Happily ever after" literature
- ▼ Parents who never fight in front of their children

▼ Parents who don't model healthy conflict resolution
▼ Pastors/teachers who imply that Christians should always agree with one another

It's nice when couples agree on things such as:

▼ What we believe
▼ Where to live
▼ How to spend our money
▼ How best to raise the kids

How many of these concepts do you and your spouse agree on? One? Maybe two? These are the very issues that most couples argue about. Do these arguments mean your marriage is on the rocks? Not necessarily.

God created men and women to complement each other. The Hebrew words translated "help meet" in the *King James Version* actually refer to a "fitting partner." In a marriage, the husband and wife are fitting partners. Think of it like a jigsaw puzzle—one piece fits another. Where one jigs, the other jags. The obvious physical aspects of fitting together are just a part of how God made men and women to be appropriate for each other. They also fit together emotionally, spiritually, and psychologically.

Good relationships are built not only on similarities, but also on differences.

What happens when two jigsaw pieces are exactly alike? They don't fit together. Good relationships are built not only on similarities, but also on differences. While people tend to enjoy being with others who are like them, they *need* to be with others who are different. The combination of *different* skills, attitudes, and tendencies creates a union that is much stronger than either individual.

When you and your spouse disagree, it may make you mad. Why can't he be more understanding? Why can't she be more logical? Doesn't he have a heart? Doesn't she have a brain?

Forgive us if these examples seem sexist. We don't mean to say one is better than the other. In fact, that's the point.

Generally speaking, women tend to be more in touch with their emotions than men. Men are often better at blocking out their emotions when they want to focus on facts. It has something to do with the fibers in our brains. You may not have that particular setup with your spouse, but many do. Many married couples are totally baffled about how the other thinks, feels, or communicates. The essence of their complaint is: Why can't my spouse be more like me?

We need to recognize our differences and honor them—and not just the gender generalities you can read in *Men Are from Mars, Women Are from Venus* or a number of other modern explorations of the sexes. You also need to recognize the unique qualities that your spouse has *individually*. Instead of railing about your spouse who talks too much, eats strange things, or buys useless objects on a whim—accept that personality quirk, learn to live with it, even prize it. Oh, you can still work to change annoying habits in your spouse—that's what negotiation is for. But understand that the differences are not a bad thing. Even arguments, fairly argued, can be healthy for your marriage. *You don't have to agree on everything.*

At one point in my marriage, my wife and I had reached an impasse on an area of disagreement. We tried talking, compromising, debating. Nothing seemed to work; we just couldn't agree.

Finally, we decided to take a piece of paper and, on one side, list all the areas we agreed on. On the other we listed the areas of disagreement. As we began our list, we went through our theology, core beliefs, family values, our priorities, the qualities we respected—our list went on and on. After filling a couple of pages we just stopped and thought about that one small area of disagreement. It seemed so silly in light of all of our commonalities. We agreed to disagree, and the issue was dropped. As far as I can remember, it never came up again. (I don't even remember what it was. That's how important the issue was!)

Today we agree to disagree on a number of issues, and our marriage is healthier for it. My wife challenges my thinking regularly and I appreciate it.

I know single men and women who make lists before they

get married—"What My Spouse Should Be." But no one has all of the qualities they are looking for, so they settle for spouses who have a number of the qualities. They assume they'll be able to change the few things that are just not right.

Are you laughing at this yet? Are you laughing because you did this very thing yourself, or because you realize how difficult it is to try to change your partner?

The fact is, those few little flaws will probably get worse. And husbands and wives begin to notice even *more* things that bother them about their partners. (People are on their best behavior when they're dating. Once married, they let it all hang out.)

If you're trying to clone your partner into someone who is like you in most ways, who thinks and feels the same things as you do—forget it. It won't happen. And it doesn't have to happen. When we let go of the clone mentality, we can relax in the knowledge that God has created our spouse to be different from us.

Apparently God likes this diversity. He uses the strengths of one partner to shore up the weaknesses in the other. If the two have strong opinions that radically differ, they can challenge each other, honing and maturing their outlooks. Maybe they'll be able to reach some middle ground on certain issues. Or maybe they'll agree to disagree. It doesn't mean the marriage is doomed.

MYTH THREE: COUPLES SHOULD LIKE THE SAME THINGS AND ENJOY THE SAME KINDS OF ACTIVITIES

Perpetrators of the myth:

▼ The dating game, trying to pick a person with similar interests
▼ Infatuation, sublimating dislike of some activities in order to be with the other person
▼ Movies and TV showing happy couples always doing lots of fun activities together
▼ Advertising hype for constant excitement

Early in my marriage, my wife and I tried to do just about everything together. She wanted me to go shopping with her and enjoy the pleasures of helping her pick out new outfits. (She also wanted to help me pick out my clothes.) I, on the other hand, wanted her to revel in the pleasures of catching fish.

Well, it didn't turn out quite as we had hoped. I was a headache that she had to drag around the mall, and she ruined my fishing trips.

This togetherness thing wasn't working—that was very obvious. But we found it hard to tell each other. How do you say to the woman you love, "I don't want you to go on my next fishing trip. It's not as much fun when you're with me"? How would she say to me, "I wish you didn't come along on my shopping trips"?

If we really loved each other, we should want to be together all of the time, right? Wrong. Sometimes one partner will enjoy doing something and the other won't. Sometimes one partner enjoys doing something on his or her own.

Sure, some people pick up new activities from their spouses. One friend of ours taught his girlfriend about baseball, and now she's a bigger fan than he is. That can happen. It's a good thing when one partner can enjoy an important activity because of the other. But it doesn't have to happen like that.

Couples need to communicate about their favorite activities. Share the things you love about fishing, golf, reading, writing, shopping, cross-stitch, canoeing, or whatever. You might even try to get the other person involved, but don't push it. Similarly, you might try to learn your spouse's favorite activities, but don't beat yourself up if you just don't enjoy them. (Also expect that there might be considerable adjustment involved as your spouse tries to involve you.)

If mutual involvement does not happen naturally, with both parties feeling good about it, drop it. There is no shame in having things you enjoy doing separately.

Today, I rarely go to the mall with my wife. And when I do, we usually split up once we get there. We have learned that we shop in very different ways. If we try to do it together, we cramp each other's style.

My wife never goes fishing with me. I have a close friend

with whom I plan several fishing excursions each year. It's a good time for me to get away, and my wife enjoys being away from me, too!

But isn't it selfish for us to need time alone? Isn't it unhealthy to spend long periods of time apart? Maybe, but not always.

It is selfish if you go off alone with no concern for your spouse. But there's nothing wrong with a person communicating a need to be alone for a period of time and the partner accepting and allowing it. In the same way, it might be unhealthy for a couple to spend so much time apart that they hardly see each other. Separate activities need to be kept in check. But reasonable periods of time apart, when both partners agree to them, may actually strengthen the times when you're together.

If mutual involvement does not happen naturally, with both parties feeling good about it, drop it. There is no shame in having things that you enjoy doing separately.

If you find that you have many separate activities, it would probably be a good idea to look for a new activity you can do together. My wife and I recently joined a tennis club. We're going to see if tennis is something we could enjoy doing together. If your separate lives are pulling you apart too often, make the effort to create good times together.

REALITY CHECK

Some couples assume they are drifting apart because the longer they're married the less they seem to enjoy doing things together. They remember the early days when they enjoyed doing so much together, but now they may be moving in very different directions. In her book *Divorce Busting*, Michele Weiner-Davis makes the point that *different* is not *bad*.

(continued on page 26)

(continued from page 25)

"There is a misconception that healthy relationships consist of two people with many mutual likes and dislikes, but this is not necessarily true. Spouses can have very diverse interests and still have a satisfying marriage. There needs to be some common ground, but not a lot. Divergent interests do not have to destroy a marriage. On the contrary, they can enhance one."[3]

MYTH FOUR: IF I FEEL NO PASSION IN THE RELATIONSHIP, THEN OUR MARRIAGE IS IN TROUBLE

COROLLARY TO MYTH FOUR: IF I FEEL PASSION FOR SOMEONE ELSE, THEN I MUST NOT BE IN LOVE WITH MY SPOUSE

Perpetrators of the myth:

▼ Our sex-saturated society, which worships passion
▼ A general tendency to equate love with feelings of being "in love"

"We used to be so in love. Life was full of passion and romance. Now he acts like he doesn't care. It seems like ages since we made love. Our marriage is in trouble if we don't breathe some new life into it soon!"

Passion and romance are strange phenomena. They are strong compulsions and hard to control. This is one area that has always perplexed me about God's creation. Why didn't He create us with the ability to sustain passion for just one person all of our lives?

Maybe you're one of the lucky ones who has always had eyes only for your spouse. Maybe you have sailed through your married life without being tempted by others. Maybe your passion for your spouse has stayed constant, even grown.

But this book is taking a realistic look at marriage, and the truth is that all marriages go through ups and downs. For many, the down times are quite low and can last a long time.

Once the infatuation stage is over and the negotiation phase begins, most couples realize that there are times when living with the same person year after year can be boring, and the lure of something new and different can be quite strong. No one should be surprised when they find their mind wandering toward something new, something different, something that seems a little more exciting. All relationships go through this strain. What keeps the marriage together? In these down times, it's not deep emotion or passion but *commitment* to one's spouse.

As Weiner-Davis describes it,

> Magic doesn't last forever. Happily married couples say magic visits from time to time, but by no means is omnipresent. When speaking of their mates these couples talk more of mutual respect, companionship, [and] friend-ship . . . than they do of magic and quiver-up-the-spine.
>
> One gets the impression that a good marriage is in many ways more like a good business partnership than the pairing of Mr. with Ms. Right. Failing to recognize the transience of magic in all relationships results in the gnawing feeling that something is wrong. Believing something is wrong with your marriage because intense feelings aren't sustained may be what's wrong with your marriage.[4]

When people come for counseling about their marriage, they often say things like the following:

> "We just don't feel the same way about each other."
> "God wouldn't want us to stay together if we don't love each other."
> "I love my spouse, but I'm no longer *in* love."
> "If I am in love with my spouse, then how can I have these feelings for someone else?"

Do any of these comments sound familiar to you? How would you respond?

We usually let clients know up front that they are going

through something most couples experience. Feelings flutter and fade, but marriage is built on commitment.

"Yes," they might say, "but aren't these feelings telling me that I've made the wrong commitment?" People talk about being "in love" with someone else. Or perhaps they're just interested in or turned on by another person. This is obviously distressing, and a serious concern for the marriage, but it is also quite common, even among Christian couples. A person may have passionate feelings toward someone other than his or her spouse. This does not mean, however, that true love has left the marriage or that the marriage is bound to end.

Most couples realize that there are times when living with the same person year after year can be boring. And the lure of something new and different can be quite strong.

An affair, whether imagined or indulged, will always be more exciting than the marriage. Why? Because it is something unknown, forbidden, and unexplored. This is probably what lies behind the intriguing biblical phrase "the lust of his eyes" (1 John 2:16). Remember that coveting made God's top ten list of human errors.

One man told me how he had "set a fleece" before God. (This is a dubious form of testing God's will that's based on a story from the biblical judge Gideon.) Here's what this man's test was: He proposed that he go away by himself for two weeks to think and pray about his wife and another woman that he was overwhelmingly attracted to. He said, "I'll see which woman I miss the most. That will determine which way I go." He reasoned that God would direct him by giving him the greatest longing for the woman he really loved.

I told him not to bother. I could predict which woman would be most on his mind—the woman who had been his obsession for the past four months. But this would have nothing to do with love and everything to do with hormones, excitement, and lust.

Some partners feel that they have to compete with these obsessions. They assume that if they could just be a little sexier, a little nicer, or a little younger looking, they could win back their mates' attention. The truth is that you cannot compete with an affair. No matter how young or sexy you are or make yourself out to be, there will always be others who have more of what you are trying to gain. And ultimately it does not come down to youth or sexiness, just *newness*. We are often attracted to something—or someone—new.

Staying together is a matter of remembering the nature of the commitment you made to your spouse. I advised the wavering husband to stay with his wife and think on that commitment. I advised his wife to give up trying to compete but to confidently remind him of the choice he made ten years ago when he promised to be her husband. (There's nothing wrong with trying to be nice or trying to make yourself look good, but that cannot be the focus of your efforts to win back your spouse.)

All marriages go through some form of temptation. Some people pursue money, career, other friendships, or even church work to fill the void of marriages that don't fulfill their expectations or needs. And many are tempted to enter extramarital romances.

An affair, whether imagined or indulged, will always be more exciting than the marriage. Why? Because it is something unknown, forbidden, and unexplored.

The question is: What do you do with the temptation?

Do you *seek* it? Some do. There are those who get tired of their marriage and go out looking for trouble. They may not even intend to "go all the way" with an illicit relationship, but they're dancing on the edge of infidelity. They want the excitement, the rush, the assurance that they're still attractive to the opposite sex. Obviously, these people are playing with fire.

Do you *entertain* temptation? You're not intending to have an affair, but there's this beautiful woman at the office, there's this nice man at school, there's this good friend at church who seems perfect for you. You find yourself comparing your spouse to that person, imagining yourself with that person, entertaining thoughts of an affair that you're not really planning to have. Meanwhile, the friendship grows more intimate. There was a spark there, and you have fanned it. You worry about where this is headed, but you console yourself with the myth: This must be right because there is passion here I've never felt in my marriage. This, too, is playing with fire. Call it what it is, a good friendship that is taking a dangerous turn. Slam on the brakes before you crash.

Do you *find strength to fight* temptation? Temptation weakens us. It snakes its way inside our souls and convinces us that we have already lost—it's useless to resist. The Tempter tries to make us feel guilty for being tempted and normal for giving in. That's backwards. It's normal to be tempted; the guilt comes when we succumb to it. So, if you are being tempted by an extra-marital affair, join the club. You're normal. You have not done anything wrong—yet. But be on your guard. Your extra-marital passion is not a sign that your marriage is doomed or that it's time to move on. It's an indication that it's time to move *back,* to renew your commitment to your marriage.

MYTH FIVE: IF WE ARE REALLY IN LOVE WE'LL KNOW EVERYTHING ABOUT EACH OTHER

Perpetrators of the myth:

- ▼ The false assumption that men and women are more alike than they really are
- ▼ Oversimplifying the spouse's personality

"After ten years of marriage he still doesn't understand how I feel. By now he should know everything about me—especially the things I need and like in our relationship. Why is it that he's so smart in other areas, but so dense when it comes to our relationship?"

Sound familiar? Couples who have been together many, many years typically exclaim, "I'm still learning new things about my wife all the time." Or, "Just when I think I have my husband all figured out, I find out that I don't know what I'm talking about."

Humans are complex beings. And we come in two flavors—male and female—which adds to the difficulties of knowing our mates completely.

Consider the following scenes:

SCENE ONE

SHE: Aren't you going to say you're sorry?
HE: For what?
SHE: Well, if you don't know, you're beyond hope.
HE: What did I do?

SCENE TWO

HE: Why did you make me go to that party?
SHE: What was wrong with it?
HE: I don't like those people. You know that.
SHE: You never told me. How was I supposed to know?
HE: Well, if you really loved me, you would just know.

SCENE THREE

SHE: I'm not getting any satisfaction out of our sex life. He just doesn't seem interested in doing the things that give me pleasure.
COUNSELOR: Have you told him what things you'd like him to do?
SHE: Well, no. I'd be embarrassed.

SCENE FOUR

HE: I'm not getting any satisfaction out of our sex life. She just doesn't seem interested in doing the things I like.
COUNSELOR: Have you told her what things you'd like her to do?
HE: Well, no. But I'm sure she knows.

These are all examples of miscommunication between partners. Do any of them sound familiar? You could probably write several more scenes yourself. The point is, your mate *can't* know things about you if you don't share them! Here's another of those gender generalizations: Women are better than men at reading minds. In general, women tune in to relationships. They learn early to read people. They pick up on subtle cues in conversation and behavior. There are many times when women *just know*.

The healthy marriage accepts changes and adjusts to them. To be happy in marriage, we cannot hold on to an ideal or expectation of how things should be — we must accept what we have.

Problems occur when wives assume that their husbands are just as perceptive as they are. They find it hard to believe that an intelligent man, who can pull off complex business deals, complete crossword puzzles, or spout off streams of sports trivia, can't figure out what he just did to hurt his wife's feelings. The truth is that often we men really are as clueless as we act.

It took my wife a while to believe this. For years I was saying that I needed her to *tell me* what she was annoyed about or what she wanted me to do. Finally, she heard the same story from other men and decided to believe me. Maybe I should take it as a compliment that she assumed I had a clue, but I really needed regular updates from her about how she was feeling, how we were doing, and what things were not going well. Otherwise, I would naively assume that all was well, and would proceed blissfully into *relationship minefields.* (You know. That's where you think everything is fine, but your partner is stewing over something, expecting you to repent of some sin you don't even know about.)

Problems also occur when husbands get too accustomed to their wives' mind-reading abilities. In many cases, men don't *have to* communicate, so they don't. They assume their wives will always *just know* what they need, because so often they *do.*

The point is, we all need to communicate. We need to speak to each other and say, right out loud, what we feel, want, and need. True love does not diminish the need for verbal communication. Love is not some Internet connection where information is automatically uploaded and downloaded. We have to talk to each other.

There is another angle to the myth, "Love means never having to say 'How are you?'" Sometimes one partner assumes he or she knows everything about the other partner. There are no more surprises, nothing left to learn.

But we are all more complex than we think, and we change over time. Hormonal changes, maturation, the cauldron of experience, all create significant adjustments in our needs, our desires, and our very identity. Just when you think you have your partner figured out, he or she may surprise you—if you're willing to be surprised. Problems occur when we don't accept the changes as they come, when we stop learning about our partners.

> SHE: But you don't like broccoli.
> HE: I thought I'd try it again. It's not so bad.
> SHE: But you don't like broccoli.

The healthy marriage accepts changes and adjusts to them. To be happy in marriage, we cannot hold on to an ideal or expectation of how things should be—we must accept what we have.

MYTH SIX: IF MY SPOUSE ISN'T WILLING TO WORK ON THE RELATIONSHIP, THEN THERE IS VERY LITTLE I CAN DO TO MAKE THINGS BETTER

Perpetrators of the myth:

- ▼ People who are in or have been in bad relationships and tell you that it doesn't get any better
- ▼ You may tell yourself this after seeing no progress over a long period of time

The divorce rate for second marriages is higher than the divorce rate for first marriages. Do people learn from their mistakes? Not usually. People tend to repeat the same problems in marriage after marriage.

Why? We call it *the blame factor.* Many of these repeat offenders are busy saying, "It's her fault!"; "If only he were . . .."; "I guess I just didn't find the right person." They're blaming their spouses when they should be looking at themselves and changing the way *they* conduct their relationships.

This is not to say that one partner should shoulder all the blame for a failed marriage. On the contrary! *Both* should take responsibility. There is no doubt that marriage works best when two people work together to make it better. In fact, whenever someone comes to us for counseling on marital issues, we try to meet with both partners. It's hard for one person to fix a relationship that involves two people.

But many times one partner (typically the man) refuses to work on the relationship or even acknowledge that there is a problem. What then? Can the other partner do anything unilaterally to save the marriage?

Within limits, yes.

There is a TV commercial that starts off with a butterfly. The narrator say something like this: "Somewhere in the Amazon forest a butterfly flaps his wings . . . which startles a leopard . . . which causes a stampede of antelope . . . which sets off a dust storm . . . which alters the weather patterns in North America. . . ."

The point is obvious. A small action can set things in motion to bring about huge changes. The same is true in our relationships. Even little actions on our part can change the whole nature of our relationships.

This is a basic premise of family systems theory: In a system when one person changes, other people will make changes in response. So *you* can make the commitment unilaterally (if necessary) to practice the techniques described in this book, to change your marriage from a power struggle to mature love. While using these techniques does not guarantee that your marriage will stay together or that your spouse will meet your needs, it will make a difference in you, and your spouse may make changes in response.

The next chapter will examine specific things you can do to bring about change. But for now you need to know that you can make a difference all by yourself. "But I'm always the one who does all the work and all of the changing." You probably also take greater responsibility in the relationship. While that might not be fair, it reflects the reality of the marriage.

Many times, one partner (usually the wife) serves as the caretaker of the relationship. When something begins to go wrong, this partner blows the whistle and demands a conference. The other partner may also be interested in preserving the relationship, but is just less observant (and probably less concerned).

If this is the case with you, accept your caretaking as a valuable role, in which you can use your God-given strengths of communication and relationship-building. Don't carp at the injustice of it, grab the opportunity. Your job is not to keep score but to do what is needed to improve the marriage.

If you work on yourself and your reactions to your spouse, two things might result. First, you will become a healthier, more mature person who is growing in faith and love. Second, your spouse may notice and make a change for the better in reaction to you. But even if the first happens without the latter result, you are still better off.

Do not work too hard to achieve the second result—positive change in your spouse. Nagging, cajoling, and guilt-mongering all tend to backfire. Put your spouse in God's hands. Be charitable and pray like crazy. But leave the changing up to your spouse and God.

SOLUTION WORKSHOP ONE

GOAL: Unmask the myths.

Research Projects

What are your marital myths? And how can you gain a more realistic view of marriage? Our first solution-based workshop is a research project of sorts. Your goal is to seek out and evaluate various opinions about marriage—in the media and among your friends.

Project one: Watch a movie together that portrays a marriage.

Discuss: What were the accurate messages you got about marriage?

What were the false messages, or myths, that you noticed?

Project two: Do the same thing with an episode of one of your favorite TV sitcoms.

Discuss: What were the accurate messages you got about marriage?

What were the false messages, or myths, that you noticed?

Project three: Interview a few of your married friends, asking them some of the following questions about the nature of their marriage. (Some may be hesitant to be honest, so it would be good to share at least one of your own difficulties in order to "prime the pump.")

▼ ▼ ▼

SAMPLE INTERVIEW FORM

1. Which statement best describes your marriage?

   ▼ Like living with your best friend
   ▼ Boring

2. If you had not married your spouse, do you think you would be happy as a single person?

3. On average, how much time do you spend each day talking to each other?

4. What hobbies or activities do you enjoy doing together? When was the last time you did one of them?

5. What different expectations did you bring to the marriage? Where did they come from?

6. a. What is different about your relationship today from the day you got married?

b. What things are better today?

c. What things are not as good?

▼　▼　▼

Project four: Select a *mentor couple*—an older couple you look up to in terms of spiritual wisdom and relational maturity. Try the same interview with them.

Review your findings and write some conclusions to the following questions.

Our Findings

1. Marriage is like. . . .

- ▼ Never-ending romance
- ▼ Living with your best friend
- ▼ Clash of the Titans
- ▼ Boring
- ▼ Other (name it):

2. What did we learn about our marriage in comparison with others?

- ▼ We're pretty normal.
- ▼ We're better off than most.
- ▼ We've got a lot of work to do.
- ▼ We wish people were more honest.
- ▼ Other (name it):

3. How realistic have our expectations about marriage been?

- ▼ We expected way too much.
- ▼ We expected things to be a bit more positive than they've been.
- ▼ Our expectations were pretty realistic from the start.
- ▼ We expected things to be a bit more negative than they've been.
- ▼ We expected too little.
- ▼ Other (name it):

4. How would it affect our marriage if we adopted more realistic expectations?

  ▼ It would take the pressure off.
  ▼ It would make us more thankful for the relationship as it is.
  ▼ It would spur us on to treat each other better.
  ▼ We would communicate more.
  ▼ We would fall madly in love with each other all over again.
  ▼ It wouldn't affect us much.
  ▼ Other (name it):

▼ ▼

CHAPTER TWO

Stages of Marriage: Where Are You?

The Princess Bride is a romantic film filled with fantasy, comedy, and adventure. At one stage in the movie the hero is dying, his life force drained from his body by the evil prince. His friends take him to Miracle Max, hoping that the wonder worker can bring their friend back to life. Max hesitates. He doubts his ability to bring this "mostly dead" young man back to life—until he asks the hero, "What is worth living for?"

The young man faintly groans, "True love." With that high purpose, the magician prepares a potion that gives the young man back his soul and heals him. The hero goes on to vanquish the evil prince and live happily ever after with his princess. This fantasy is funny and romantic, but its popularity speaks to the basic belief that most of us have grown up with—out there somewhere is the right one for me, and, if I can only find that person, I will be healed, fully alive, and whole.

Bob and Diane had been married only four years when they came to my* office for marital therapy. He was a salesman, and she was taking time off from her career to care for their infant daughter at home. They described their courtship and early marriage as full of love and romance. At first they seemed to meet each other's needs perfectly, enjoying a mutual sense of oneness

*All first person pronouns in this chapter refer to Tom Bartlett.

emotionally and sexually. But now Diane was complaining that Bob was more distant. During the months prior to this visit, he didn't want to go out and do things as much as he had before. Even worse, he had become less attentive to her needs.

Bob said that he felt pressure to work harder to provide for the family. Instead of encouragement, he only felt more pressure about not having time to spend together. Suddenly Diane seemed to get angry over the least little things. Bob didn't know what to do.

Most couples operate under the assumption that marrying the right person and finding romance will heal every wound, smooth every bump, and eliminate every difference between them.

By the time they got to my office, both were thinking about divorce. They wondered out loud if their marriage would last. Had they married the right person?

They talked about how they met and fell in love, then how distant and hurt they felt in their relationship. The pain of disappointment at lost romance was intense. Like most couples I see in therapy, they operated under the assumption that marrying the right person and finding romance would heal every wound, smooth every bump, and eliminate every difference between them. When they found out each had blemishes previously unseen and the other had needs to be met instead of an untiring desire to meet *their own* needs, the glow faded. Hope and joy turned to disappointment, then resentment. Union turned to conflict. How could this be?

All marriages go through natural stages. A couple must progress through these stages to achieve a long-lasting and mutually satisfying love relationship. However, as in the case of Bob and Diane, many couples don't understand the normal stages of marriage. We have been taught that love is magical and mysterious, passionate and eternally blissful. Some of the most well-known literature and music in recorded history deal with romantic love. The most enduring of them demonstrates a passion that flies in the face of cultural differences, and in the face of reason or good judgment, with tragic results—*Romeo and Juliet.* But somehow the tragic results never outweigh the brief flutter of immortal love. True love is worth it all (or so we've been told).

From stories like "Cinderella," we learn at a very young age that "someday my prince will come," or "I'll find the one whose foot fits the glass slipper." We grow up believing that the hard part is in the finding or the waiting; somehow, once that is completed, the work is over. Unfortunately these expectations do not bode well for creating marriages that are strong, healthy, loving, or long lasting. It's the day *after* the prince comes that the work of true love begins. We must recognize that the joy and love of a marriage relationship grows through time *as we struggle through certain relational stages.*

> *All marriages go through natural stages. A couple must progress through these stages to achieve a long-lasting and mutually satisfying love relationship.*

What are these stages, and how can understanding them help you restore your marriage? There seem to be three fairly distinct stages in marriage—the infatuation (or romantic) stage, the negotiation stage (or power struggle), and finally the stage of mature love (or mutual interdependence).[1]

THE INFATUATION STAGE

This is the stage in which romance abounds! When we try to define romance, most of us would concur with the dictionary: "marked by or constituting passionate love." But dictionaries also describe *romantic* as "having no basis in fact" and "impractical in conception or plan." Romance has been described as being "head over heels" or "madly in love." The stage of infatuation is the stage in which we feel the exhilaration of emotion and a sense of oneness with our partner. There is a feeling of having finally found the *one for me.* In the midst of this stage,

STAGES OF MARRIAGE

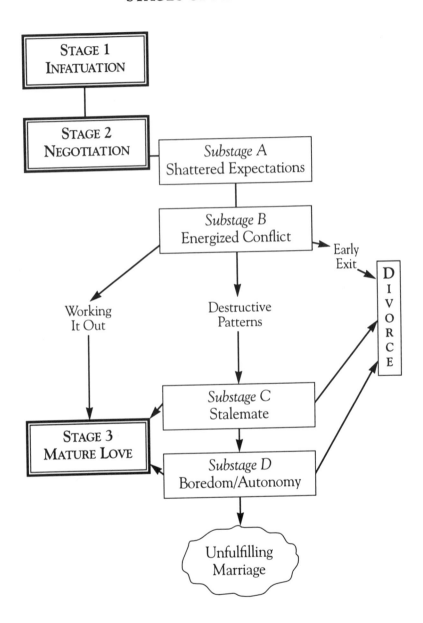

partners seem to meet each other's needs fully, without demands for change or accommodation. The intensity of attraction seems to be at its summit. Most of our favorite love stories and music focus on this stage of the relationship.

In *Getting the Love You Want*, Harville Hendrix indicates that four sentences encompass what lovers in the infatuation stage have said for all time:

> "I know we just met, but somehow I feel as though I already know you."
>
> "Even though we've only been seeing each other for a short period of time, I can't remember when I didn't know you."
>
> "When I'm with you, I no longer feel alone; I feel whole, complete."
>
> "I love you so much, I can't live without you."[2]

These sentences, Hendrix writes, summarize the needs and fears we bring to marriage in our search for wholeness. He describes romantic love as an illusion in which couples have to appear "to be more emotionally healthy than they really are."[3] We become so focused on being cared for that we ignore the blemishes or neediness of our partner. At the same time we attempt to present ourselves as *unneedy* in order to remain attractive to our partner. Romantic love has been described as "a delusional state in a normal, healthy human being. It is based 90+% on projection of one's own inner idealized version of the other, rather than an accurate perception of him or her."[4]

Romantic love has been described as "a delusional state in a normal, healthy human being."

Think about what a first date is like. You get all dressed up in your best outfit. You fix your hair just right, and put on your best smelly stuff. You make sure your house or your car is impeccably clean. Then you make reservations at your favorite restaurant, anticipating the ideal mood, music, and witty conversation. The presentation is clear: "This is the real me! I'm always like this. In fact, I wake up every morning just as you see me now!" Of course it's a false impression.

So if the romantic stage is a time when we're not thinking realistically, when we don't see the blemishes in our spouses or show the blemishes in ourselves, and if romance inevitably fades away—what is its purpose? Is romance a trickster that promises us "happily ever after," only to leave us feeling foolish, stupid, and disappointed?

We don't think so.

Romance is a wonderful and delicious period, and it does have a purpose: to allow for the bonding and attachment necessary for a healthy marriage to take place. It gives the opportunity for two people who indeed are different to come together long enough to develop strong enough attachments that when the scales finally come off the eyes and the blemishes and neediness of our partners become visible, the bonds have been established that will allow us to work on ourselves and the marriage. We don't need to do away with romance, but we should understand its purpose. We must remember that it is transient—a stage we move *through* and do not stay in.

As we saw in the previous chapter, many of us have wrong ideas about romance. To name a few:

1. Intensity of romance is the best indicator of the health of your relationship.
2. If you are with the right person, you will stay in romantic love forever.
3. If you are truly in love, the other person will know your needs without even asking.
4. If there is no passion in your relationship, then you must not be in love.

Bob and Diane started their marriage with these myths. But very quickly, they each began to sense the disappointment of being married to someone who had different needs, who expected the other to change, and so on. All of a sudden they began to ask, "Did I marry the right person?" and "Can this marriage last?" This growing awareness that one's partner does not exist to meet every need—that our idealized view of marriage does not match the reality of experience—leads into the second primary stage of marriage, the power struggle, the stage of negotiation.

THE NEGOTIATION STAGE

Not long after a couple makes a commitment to spend their lives together, the bright, white-hot light of romance begins to fade. What happens to dull this bright light of love? Why does the *oneness*—knowing what the other is thinking or feeling without words being expressed—suddenly change into confusion, conflict, and disappointment?

Marriage is a process of bringing together two individuals and in the process of coming together and working through their differences, there are bound to be struggles for power and control. One marriage expert says, "The long-term intimate couple relationship is one of the few in our culture to which adults can turn with a feeling of security, and have their child nurturant needs met. At the same time, [there is] the need to feel oneself to be independent, [and] self-directing."[5]

We look to our marriage relationship to meet our needs— especially our needs for security and safety—but at the same time we have the need to be independent and competent. Our conflicting needs make for a rather complex process, one that we can divide into four substages: *shattered expectations, energized conflict, stalemate,* and *boredom/autonomy.*

Shattered Expectations
When a couple begins to realize *the honeymoon is over,* they enter the transitional stage of marriage. Most couples begin their marriage with huge expectations, and revising them is painful. Marital myths die hard, and the delirium of the infatuation stage usually gives way to a collection of negative emotions—anger, frustration, disappointment, depression—as a couple thuds back to reality.

As we have indicated, several of the most common marital

myths are based on the assumption that spouses are more alike than different. During the dating process couples routinely seek out their points of commonality and ignore major points of difference. Even when there are obvious differences, couples tend to view them as complementary—"You're the perfect match for me because you're everything I'm not." Both partners tend to downplay their *me* attitudes and celebrate the *us*.

When infatuation fades, both partners begin to realize that they're married to strangers. They really don't have as much in common as they thought. In fact, they're different, and those differences begin to grate on them.

Let's say two people—Jack and Mary—meet at a party and hit it off well. *Very* well. They're seeing stars and hearing bells and feeling goose pimples. Suddenly Jack says, "Let's go."

"Where?" Mary responds.

"Anywhere. Let's go on a trip. Go home and pack your bags. I'll meet you at the airport tomorrow."

Of course, Mary is so enamored that she agrees without hesitation.

Marriage is something like this. You and your partner agree to go on a life-long journey together after knowing each other only a relatively short time. But where are you going? What baggage are you bringing along?

Mary arrives at the airport lugging suitcases full of swimsuits and scuba gear. She assumes they're going to an exotic island resort. That's *her* idea of an ideal vacation. But Jack has his fur-lined parka and hiking boots, all geared up for a wilderness adventure in the Yukon. That's *his* idea of a great getaway.

So it is with marriage. In exhilarating moments of discovery, people can easily overlook how different they are from their future partners, suppressing the *me* in favor of the wonderful new *us* that's developing. They embark on their journey with different interests, different expectations, and different baggage.

Let's look briefly at three major areas of difference.

1. Opposites attract. There needs to be a certain amount of common interest for a romance to get off the ground, but many of us are attracted to people who contrast with us in personality or interests or opinions. It's as if we're seeking someone to *complete* us, to fill in the qualities that we lack. But these same *complementary* qualities can cause great problems later.

Diane was attracted to Bob because of his stability and predictability, just as Bob's attraction to Diane was fostered by his sense that she was spontaneous, creative, and unpredictable. The differences, which often foster attraction during the romantic stage, can become a source of conflict during the negotiation stage. The stable and unflappable Bob becomes predictable, boring, and unmotivated. The energetic Diane, creative and unpredictable, becomes disorganized, undependable, and impulsive. At an even more basic level, Diane used to love spending the day fishing with Bob because she had him all to herself. Now that the romantic glow is gone, she realizes she never really liked fishing. Bob used to love spending the day walking around the mall with Diane; but now he'd just as soon go to the dentist.

Their basic personality differences serve to underscore the new thoughts racing through their minds: "We are not alike. We are not the perfect match. So what are we doing together?"

2. There are also basic inherent differences between men and women, particularly in the area of communication, that tend to lead to misunderstanding and conflict. Men and women are different. That's no secret. But when we forget the differences in our everyday interaction, problems arise. Men and women essentially speak different languages, yet they often blame each other for the lack of communication. Here's a classic example.

The wife says, "I love my husband, but he doesn't seem to love me anymore."

The husband says, "I love my wife, but she doesn't seem to love me anymore."

What do they each mean? Let's examine the situation.

How does the husband express his love for his wife? By making sure that the car is filled with gas and serviced so she doesn't have to and so she is safe on the road.

What expression is she looking for? She wants him to say, "I love you." He loves her all right, but he's not a verbal kind of guy. Like so many men, he would rather *do* something than talk about it.

How does the wife express her love for her husband? By

talking with him about her feelings for him and asking about his feelings.

What expression is he looking for? Well, he wants her to be interested in what he says about his sales meeting. He wants her to be proud of him for his success at work. Oh, she loves him, but she finds all of that sales talk pretty boring.

The two define love in very different ways.

Later, we'll look at gender differences in more detail and discuss how to overcome them, but the following list may give you a preliminary understanding of the general differences in the communication styles of men and women.

A. Men tend to be *solution-* and *achievement-oriented* in relation to problems, while women tend to focus on the *feelings* and *relationship* issues involved. Thus women tend to remember details about a conversation and their feelings about it, while men tend to remember only the bottom line.

B. Men tend to be socialized more toward *competition* and *independence* and therefore tend to try to solve problems without help from others. Women tend to be more *open* with others and thus they *share feelings* in order to solve problems. Men use *I language*; women use *we language*.

C. In relationships, women tend to associate *talking* (and sharing feelings) with greater intimacy, while men tend to make connections through *activity*, and generally think, *If we need to talk, something must be wrong.*

Recently a couple was in my office discussing, among other things, their frustrations with how a friend had treated their children. Both agreed that the friend's behavior had hurt their children's feelings. In fact, they agreed on virtually every detail about the situation. But it remained a source of conflict between the two of them. Why?

The husband had a problem to solve, and he came up with a solution—ignore it. He determined that the problem would only get worse if they took stronger action, and it would probably go away by itself. But the wife continued to complain about it. As the husband saw it, his wife was undermining his problem-solving ability. But as the wife saw it, her husband was ignoring her feelings. She wanted him to identify with her feelings of hurt and frustration for her children rather than simply to find a solution.

They finally were able to resolve the conflict only after they began to see the situation through each other's eyes. She needed to develop a more solution-oriented approach. He needed to understand the emotional issues and support his wife's feelings.

3. *The most enduring differences that you and your spouse bring to marriage come from your families of origin.* You each have childhood issues that continue to impact how you feel and how you relate to others. It might be something said or done by your parents, siblings, teachers, or schoolmates, but it affects the way you see yourself and how you deal with current situations. You don't have to solve all your nagging personal issues in order to have a good marriage, but you do need to understand how they affect you—and how your spouse's issues affect your spouse. You both look at life through different lenses, lenses that have been ground by a lifetime of experiences. As you work through the negotiation stage of your marriage, you must not expect your spouse to see through your lens.

Bob and Diane, for instance, brought issues and expectations related to the behavior of their parents, their parents' marriages, the role they each played in their family, and so forth, all of which affected their own emotional strengths and needs.

Bob was the second youngest of four brothers. His parents had been married for thirty years when he married Diane. His father had worked at the same job all of his life, and his parents had a relatively affectionate and stable marriage. Bob had experienced some serious health problems early in his life, which created an especially strong bond between him and his mother. His mother and father both had very traditional roles in the family.

Diane's parents, by contrast, divorced when she was in elementary school. She was the oldest of two children and remembers her parents having a great deal of conflict. Both of her parents worked outside of the home and, after the divorce, Diane lived with her mom until she graduated from college. Her father took a job out of the state, so he was never able to pay her enough attention. Diane described herself as having a hard time trusting people. She was afraid that any conflict would destroy a relationship and had always prided herself on not rocking the boat. She worked very hard at pleasing others.

When Bob and Diane met during Bob's sophomore year at college, the attraction was immediate and intense. Each was sure that the other person was the *right one*. We don't want to simplify things too much, but it seems that Diane was desperate to find a man she could depend on and please, while Bob wanted a girl—as the song goes—"just like the girl who married dear old Dad." At first, each seemed to meet the other's need. But their needs carried some impossible expectations with them, which was bound to create conflict. Their expectations had to shatter.

One respected author notes,

> There could hardly be a couples therapist who would claim not to have noticed how a childhood experience has a tendency to be repeated or defended against in subsequent relationships with partners. This is a transferential aspect of a couple's relationship. Early experiences of a cruel father lead to expectations of repetitions of, or determined attempts to avoid, neutralize, or deny cruelty in a husband. The man who grew up with an alcoholic mother who never listened to his feelings marries a diet-obsessed Valium addict, who is too absorbed in her own distress management to pay attention to his emotional needs. Equally, the patterns of child abandonment or neglect tend to be feared or apparently repeated in a heart lurchingly predictable manner (despite the most stringent attempts to avoid it).[6]

Whether our family-of-origin issues are as significant as abuse or alcoholism or more subtle, such as low self-esteem or performance pressure, we all come to marriage with needs replayed from our childhood, and most of us expect marriage to meet our needs. This is what makes the stage of shattered expectations so difficult. We have two sets of needs and need-based expectations.

Needs often propel a relationship, bringing two people together quickly, with some sort of mystical *chemistry.* But the expectations based on these needs often make it difficult for a couple to get past the infatuation stage. It seems that the greater the need, the more strongly held the ideal, the higher is the expectation of having the spouse meet that need. If those expectations are not modified, couples tend to hold tenaciously to the myths and, therefore, assume they have married the wrong person.

"US" AND "ME" IMPULSES IN THE STAGES OF MARRIAGE

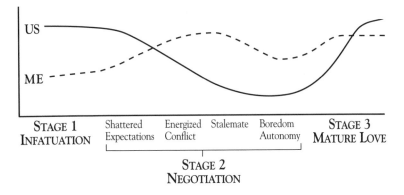

ENERGIZED CONFLICT

The second substage within the *negotiation stage* is marked by disagreement. A new tension emerges—between *us* and *me.* Up to this point, the partners have been caught up in each other, giving freely of themselves to make their romance work. Then they begin to realize that they aren't getting all their needs met—they've been working hard to meet the *other's* needs. Now both face the threat of losing bits of their own identities, so they begin to get a little selfish.

They are still committed to the marriage, at least at first, but they are both pulling the marriage in their own directions.

As differences—of opinion, of background, of taste, of communication styles—become clearer, this tug of war can grow very intense.

"This marriage would be great if she would only learn to do things my way."

"We'd be so happy if he would realize that I'm right."

In the stage of energized conflict, each partner's position is, "I want *us* to make our marriage work but on *my* terms." This stage can last ten years or more but is usually most intense in years two to five of a marriage.

At this point couples tend to choose one of three paths.

1. Divorce. Some are so overwhelmed by this struggle that they end the marriage. In a recent issue of the American Psychological Association *Monitor*, marital research was reviewed, including an in-depth study of sixty couples. This study by psychologist Tom Bradbury was designed to find factors behind couples splitting up or staying together. The article's author, Beth Azar, quotes Bradbury as stating, "Most marriages end within the first five to seven years, with the brunt of instability occurring in the first two to five years. Over time a spouse realizes that his or her partner isn't nurturing or supportive and becomes resentful."[7] In other words, *us* has turned to *me*. *I* am not getting what *I* need from *us*. I am giving more than I'm getting. Ironically, both partners often feel that same way.

Many people who divorce, are surprised by the level of conflict in marriage, expecting the romantic stage to continue their whole lives. They fail to negotiate anything because they think they shouldn't have to. As they see it, conflict indicates that they married the wrong person.

2. Destructive patterns. Other couples find their conflicts confusing, but are committed to staying together. They didn't expect marriage to be so hard, and they're not prepared to deal with their differences. Once again, the *me* impulse supersedes the *us* impulse, and both parties fight for their own way. As a result, various destructive patterns develop (see chapter 7). Instead of creating safety for each other, both try to gain the upper hand. If the partners are passive-aggressive or passive by nature, this raging battle may not be open, loud, or violent—

but it still seethes under the surface. Couples taking this path tend to stay stuck in the power struggle, moving on to the sub-stages of stalemate and of boredom and autonomy.

3. *Working it out.* Some are able to recognize that the con-flict they experience, while unpleasant at times, is quite normal. They know they need to work things out, and so they do, learn-ing to communicate and compromise. They may hit some bumps in the road, but keep moving forward. Career changes, the arrival of children, illness, the departure of children—these can all cause temporary problems, but couples can work them out. Ultimately they reach the mature love stage with a few bumps and bruises but are rather healthy overall.

What happened to the *me* and *us* impulses? Both are still there, in tension. The seeming selflessness of the romantic stage is replaced with a healthier view of oneself and one's own needs. But when couples work things out, they learn to give and take. Negotiation is the perfect word for it, because it can be as mer-cantile as any business dealing—"I'll drive Johnny to soccer practice today but then you cook dinner tomorrow." The *me* and *us* impulses are both present, but neither one dominates.

STALEMATE

In the substage following conflict, the partners are just plain tired. They've been fighting so long, they just don't have the energy for it anymore. Whatever hopes or dreams they brought into the marriage have been shattered by their constant bickering.

"She just doesn't get it."

"He'll never change."

"This marriage will never be what I hoped it would be. How could I have been so naive?"

Some take the divorce route at this point, but most are still heavily invested in the relationship. Maybe they stay together for the kids or for financial reasons. Or maybe they still—down deep—love each other, though they have a hard time showing it.

When do people reach the stalemate stage? It depends how much energy they have. Some can stay in energized conflict for ten years; others get tired after three. Most couples start settling into their stalemate stage around years five to seven. (The fabled *seven-year itch* is probably related to this stage.)

In this stage they don't fight as much, but they're not as intimate either. Certain subjects are avoided in conversation because neither one wants to get involved in another fight. A strange kind of comfort level develops as they learn to tiptoe around each other.

Their strong-willed *me* impulses have flagged a little, but the *us* impulses have dropped off even more. They begin to develop separate lifestyles, and they release each other to do so. Instead of going to a movie together, he'll go bowling while she goes to the mall. They still do some things together, especially socially, but they also develop separate groups of friends with whom they may spend more time.

This kind of marriage is not necessarily on the rocks. In fact, we find that such couples are star pupils in therapy. They are tired of fighting, and they know they need help. As they learn to address their safety issues and seek some solutions to their stalemate, they can progress to the stage of mature love.

However, if they don't do something to change the course of their slow drifting away from each other, they are likely to continue to live separate lives together and move on to the next substage: *boredom and autonomy.*

BOREDOM AND AUTONOMY
"The only difference between a rut and a grave is the dimensions."[8] The statement holds true for a lot of marriages. During the stalemate stage, unless something is done to reawaken interest in the marriage, the *us* impulse keeps sliding and sliding until it nearly flatlines. This can happen anywhere from ten to thirty years into the marriage. (A number of people in mid-life crisis find a sudden surge in their *me* impulse, but they realize their *us* impulse has been dormant for a while. Sometimes they try to reinvigorate the marriage, and sometimes they leave it.)

In this stage, the partners seem to live parallel lives. They develop separate interests and involvements, appearing together occasionally for social events, at church, or for the kids' sake, but there is no real participation in each other's lives. The relationship is boring and not worth developing.

Why do they stay together? It's easier. They fit each other like old shoes, even though they hardly talk. They have established their systems of coexistence and have grown used to them. They are in their grave—oops! I mean, *rut*—and it's hard to climb out.

Sadly, some stay in this substage for the rest of their lives. Others jump ship in mid-life, divorcing to pursue some new, exciting relationship. Still others get tired of it and seek counseling to breathe new life into their marriage. It *is* possible to progress to the stage of mature love from this point, but it takes some sustained energy.

IS THERE HOPE FOR YOU?

After reading this section, you may think all marriages are doomed. How can people who are so different take those differences and turn them into mature, long-lasting, and fulfilling love relationships? As difficult as it seems, it is not out of reach.

One of my favorite quotes from M. Scott Peck comes from a taped lecture he gave called "Further Along the Road Less Traveled." In it, he described his own turbulent marriage and the constant conflict he and his wife were experiencing. He shared with the crowd that about five years into his marriage, he and his wife hit bottom. He got angry with his wife, began to withdraw from her, and finally started caring about her less. She reciprocated by not caring about him.

As Dr. Peck put it, "You know what I mean when I say we stopped caring about each other? I mean that I gave up trying to change and control her life, and she gave up trying to change or control me. *And our marriage has been steadily improving ever since!*"[9]

The journey toward mature love begins as we recognize the following:

1. In spite of the differences we bring to marriage, there are significant similarities in our basic needs that provide a point of common ground on which to build a

healthy marriage. We want to maintain our independence but at the same time experience safety, acceptance, and unconditional love.

2. Neither of us intends to hurt the other. Sometimes it may *seem* intentional, but that's because we are afraid that we aren't getting the safety, acceptance, and unconditional love we need. We seek to protect ourselves, and in that process may end up hurting each other.

3. We recognize the need to make this marriage a safe haven for both of us and are willing to learn about each other and identify our individual needs.

4. Different is not necessarily bad. Many of the differences we bring to this marriage are complementary. We are willing to face and struggle with our differences *together* in such a way that safety, connection, contact, and warmth are increased.

THE MATURE LOVE STAGE

In *Private Lies*, Frank Pitman quips, "Marriage partners are not made in heaven but are a product of on-the-job training."[10] Mature love is described as a stage of mutual interdependence. To develop a mature love, you must accept the difficult challenge of creating a good marriage. It's not a matter of *finding* the right person — mature love involves *being* the right person.

You must take responsibility for communicating your needs and desires to your partner rather than assuming that your partner automatically knows them. Flexibility is also important. You have to have the ability to recognize what is not working and allow yourself to find other ways of dealing with the problem. And through it all, you need to be solidly committed to your mate. How important is that person to you? Important enough to get you working through problems rather than trying to ignore them?

The stage of mature love does not mean the end of all conflict. Far from it! Marriage is like a garden. As you get to know a garden, you recognize different plants and appreciate the uniqueness of each one. You also recognize the weeds, and you pull them out before they can damage the other plants.

By the time they reach the mature stage, couples have learned to appreciate each other's uniqueness. But they can't just sit back and bask in the beauty of love as if all their work is done. They also recognize the "weeds" of the relationship — petty arguments, jealousies, attitudes that can creep up and choke the life out of the relationship. Couples at this stage are better at tending the garden, picking weeds before they become major problems, and spreading the nourishment of safety, respect, and solid communication.

▼   ▼   ▼

Where are you now? Which stage do you find yourself in? Probably the middle stage, negotiation, or one of its substages. Perhaps you feel that you married the wrong person. The temptation is strong to go back to the romantic stage with someone else. We find that to be the case whenever we conduct one of our divorce recovery seminars. Many participants describe the frustration of lost romance and the exhilaration they feel when someone new comes along.

This is no surprise. As romantic love fades away, and you move into the next stage of the relationship, extra-marital relationships are naturally a strong enticement. But for those who want a lasting, growing, and more intimate love, there must be a commitment to move forward — together — through the difficult times.

We're guessing that you want to keep your marriage together. How can you improve your marriage? How can you move beyond the power struggle? How can you free yourself from the cycle of conflict or suffocation of stalemate?

The rest of this book is designed to help you negotiate the differences, the communication styles, and the defensiveness that characterize the power struggle, and to help you move to the stage of mature love. Two key areas will start you on the road: a decision to focus on solutions for your marital problems and a commitment to making the marriage safe.

Solutions. Finding solutions is not about assessing blame. That won't do much good. It's not about winning or losing. The objective is to make your marriage better. Will you decide to pursue this goal?

Safety. You also need to commit as a couple to make your marriage *safe*. Can you work through the stages in ways that allow for expressions of disagreement but in ways that avoid the sabotage and open warfare that wound each other more? Bob and Diane were able to make such a commitment, which allowed them the ability to look at themselves and their marriage honestly. They have been able to move from separation to satisfaction.

SOLUTION WORKSHOP TWO

GOAL: Assess which stage of marriage you are in.

Husband: Put an "**✗**" on the spot on the graph that you believe best represents where your marriage is.

Wife: Put an "**✔**" on the spot on the graph that you believe best represents where your marriage is.

"US" AND "ME" IMPULSES IN THE STAGES OF MARRIAGE

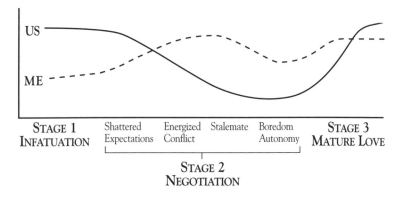

1. How did your marriage begin?

2. Describe characteristics of your relationship during the romantic phase: your communication, your feelings for one another, and how you treated each other during that time.

3. When did you know the honeymoon was over? Was there an event or a time period which showed you that the bubble had burst?

4. Name one good thing about the stage or substage you think you're in. (Examples: *Energized Conflict*—It's clear that we both care about the marriage. *Stalemate*—We know how to coexist with each other.)

5. Name one thing you'd like to change about the stage or substage you're in.

6. What can you do to move forward? How will you begin to do this?

CHAPTER THREE

Focusing on Solutions

An old vaudeville routine goes like this:

Patient: Doc, it hurts when I do this!
Doctor: Then don't do that!

We expect medical doctors to offer better advice than that. We want them to heal the underlying problem. If the patient is frustrated with a difficult marriage, and the doctor is a psychological counselor, the same conversation might sound like this:

Patient: Doc, it hurts when I argue with my husband.
Doctor: Then don't argue with your husband.

Could the solution ever be that easy? For decades, the psychological community has said no. It is necessary, the experts have said, to dig up the underlying causes of your problems — your upbringing, your toilet training, your playground failures, your first love. Marital problems, for instance, might be just the tip of a massive iceberg of personal woes.

As a result, many people have spent years in therapy, gaining oodles of insight into why they do what they do and feel what they feel — but they never translate it into behavioral change. Maybe there's a new joke here:

Patient: Doc, it hurts when I do this!
Doctor: That's because your mother hit you when you
    were a child.
Patient: Yeah, but it still hurts when I do this!

Does it truly help to excavate unconscious motives if you never change the behaviors that brought you to the counselor's office?

I* attended a national conference where Michele Weiner-Davis presented basic principles of a new counseling strategy known as solution-based therapy (SBT). She showed several taped counseling sessions in which a troubled couple made remarkable progress in just three sessions.

As I watched the video, I was impressed with how quickly these new techniques were working. The couple came in barely able to speak to each other without interrupting and shouting. They rated their marriage as very poor and didn't expect it to get much better. By the third session they were in love again. They held hands as they sat on the sofa, spoke kindly to each other, and rated their marriage as being much better than it was before. Amazingly, they ended the session by saying that they felt they didn't need counseling anymore. They would call if they got into trouble again.

The speaker then opened the session for questions and comments from the audience. After several accolades from the crowd, one astute psychologist made the following observation: "You know, when the couple first came in, I noticed the woman was twitching her leg the whole time she was talking. Then, I saw the same behavior in the second session. Finally, in the last session, even though the couple reported tremendous success, I noticed that the wife was still twitching her leg vigorously. Isn't that an indication of an underlying problem that you completely overlooked in your therapy?"

I remember feeling badly that the speaker was thrown such a curve ball, but Weiner-Davis didn't skip a beat. "The couple came in to work on their marital communication," she said, "so

*All first person pronouns in this chapter refer to Tom Whiteman.

that's what I treated. The woman never identified 'foot twitching behaviors' as part of her treatment goal. If she ever comes in for that issue, I'd be glad to help her."

Solution-based therapy makes a lot of sense. Sure, there are often underlying problems that wreak havoc in a marriage, but these are usually deeply buried. By the time they are dug up and dealt with, the marriage may be over. Many marriages need help *now*. The partners need ways to change their behaviors, find solutions, and live together in harmony.

A CIRCULAR PROBLEM

Bill and Patti entered their marriage — the second for each — a little older and a little wiser. Or so they thought. Each had been burned in a previous marriage that only lasted a few years. Before remarrying they had taken their time and been selective to make sure the next marriage would last, unwilling to go through the pain of another divorce.

At first they found excitement in talking about almost anything. For Patti, Bill was like an oasis in a desert since her first husband rarely communicated. For Bill, who had dated off and on, Patti was the woman he had been looking for: the woman he could share his life with.

When they first got married, romance and intimacy flourished. But as Bill worked to build his business, the hectic schedule took his focus away from home more and more. When Bill got home, he would crash on the sofa, exhausted. Then, when Patti tried to talk with him, Bill showed very little interest. This reminded Patti of her first husband, which made her panic, thinking, "He doesn't love me anymore!" or "We're going to end up divorced!"

Patti reacted by shutting down emotionally. She felt that she needed to protect herself from getting hurt. Bill assumed that Patti was growing cold because she was no longer attracted to him, which revived memories of his ex as well. Distance grew and intimacy declined, but neither one knew what to do to turn things around. They both protected themselves yet longed for something better.

When they finally came to me for counseling, it seemed like it was their last shot at saving the marriage. They had not been intimate with each other in months and the tension between them was almost visible. She started the first session by complaining about his job, how it took him away from her and used up all his energy so that he had nothing left for her when he came home.

He pointed out how he had to make a living and how he expected her to be a little more supportive as he worked on his business. He went on to explain that her job was almost as draining as his, that she was often exhausted herself, and that she had no right to point a finger at him. He ended his side of the story by saying that if he had something worth coming home to, like a little affection, then maybe he'd be more motivated to leave work early once in a while.

> *It takes time to uncover past hurts and unresolved conflicts. Meanwhile the partners are hanging on to the marriage by a thread.*

While the details may be a little different, this scenario has been played out over and over in my office, and perhaps in your home. The arguments are circular: "I did this because you did that." "Yeah, but I wouldn't have done that if it hadn't been for the fact that you did this first." In the same way the chicken-or-the-egg argument asks which came first, as the counselor I am called upon to pronounce the first offense.

In a more traditional approach than solution-based therapy, a counselor might begin to explore why this couple is in so much pain, tracing the beginnings of the conflict, going back to their families of origin and their first marriages.

This approach wouldn't be wrong. A great deal of good might come out of such exploration, but it would certainly take time. It takes time to uncover past hurts and unresolved conflicts. In the meantime the marriage might not change at all. In some cases, the marriage deteriorates even further as both partners bring up very difficult issues. The counselor might respond with a statement like this: "Sometimes things have to get worse before they can get better." Meanwhile the partners are hanging on to the marriage by a thread.

With the focus on solutions, counselors take a very different tactic. "Who cares how it all got started? The more important question now is, 'What are we going to do about it?'"

FOCUS ON SOLUTIONS

Applying solution-based therapy to the example of Bill and Patti, we would not investigate how the problems started, nor focus on the underlying hurts and unmet needs. Instead we would ask the couple about what kind of marriage they would like to have. Then we'd talk about what it would take specifically to get there.

Marriages have strengths as well as weaknesses. Many couples have problems with fighting, but they know how to make up. They have experienced good times as well as the bad times. That means they have the tools to make their marriage better.

You have the tools to make your marriage better. Solution-based therapy is a matter of finding those tools and sharpening them. The tools, which we'll discuss later in more depth, include listening, expressing your emotions, controlling your anger, negotiating, and giving the benefit of the doubt.

One solution-based therapy technique is *the miracle question.* I ask a couple: "Imagine that after you go to bed tonight God does a miracle in your life. He heals your marriage. He makes it the kind of marriage that you're looking for and that honors Him. When you wake up in the morning, what would be different, and how would you know that a miracle had happened?"

Most couples respond to this question by describing their ideal relationship. They would notice the difference right away, they say, because their spouse is interested in them, responsive to their needs, and so on. Notice that the focus is on the other person, what that person does differently.

The couples' responses often lead me to this follow-up question: "How would *you* be different as a result of this miracle?" This question leads to a discussion of goals that the couple might set in order to achieve their ideal.

GOAL ORIENTATION

In order to measure progress and change, the couple needs to identify specific goals they would like to accomplish over the next few weeks (short-term goals) and then specific goals they would like to accomplish over five to ten years (long-term objectives).

In the case of Bill and Patti, as much as they wanted to argue and complain about each other, the miracle question got them talking about what they would like to see in their marriage — a positive focus — and the goal setting got them to focus on solutions.

You have the tools to make your marriage better. Solution-based therapy is a matter of finding those tools and sharpening them.

The goals need to be very concrete, measurable, and balanced. Making them concrete and measurable means that when one person expresses a goal like "I want to feel loved," I try to clarify by asking, "What would it take for you to feel loved?" If the wife has three goals, then the husband should come up with three.

For Bill and Patti, their initial goals were:

BILL	PATTI
1. Greater intimacy — talking at least twenty minutes per day	1. Greater intimacy — making love at least once a week
2. To work only two evenings per week	2. Support Bill's work by showing interest in it and encouraging him
3. Go out at least one night a week for a nice dinner or movie	3. When we go out, we need to have fun; therefore, I'll avoid bringing up problem areas on our dates

Notice that their goals are very similar. They both want support, love, and affirmation; they just have different ways of achieving them.

These goals are an initial step. My job as counselor is to hold them accountable to accomplish these goals and then to move them forward toward even more ambitious changes. The key to successful accomplishment may lie in Bill and Patti's ability to encourage one another toward a stronger relationship.

A POSITIVE APPROACH

It is crucial to maintain a very positive focus while working through the restoration process. Couples will need some patience and persistence—there will be some setbacks along the way—*but they are making progress!* This positive focus starts from the moment they sit down in the counselor's office.

Traditionally, they would be asked for their *presenting problem.*

"What seems to be the trouble here?"

"What are you struggling with?"

"What's wrong with your marriage?"

That, of course, sets them off on simultaneous tirades about what's wrong, when the trouble started, and whose fault it is. The focus is on the negatives. It's sometimes amazing that couples make it through the first session.

But in solution-based therapy, I would take a decidedly positive approach:

"Tell me what's working in your marriage."

"Where would you like to see your marriage go?"

"How can I help you?"

Such positive questions often surprise couples who see me. They don't expect to talk about what's good about their relationship. But what a difference it makes! The whole focus of the hour is changed when the couple starts to identify things that are working.

I worked with one couple off and on for a few years—they called me whenever they had a big argument. I would ask them what had happened and they would recall, blow by blow, their argument. This erupted into a replaying and re-arguing of the entire incident, which could often take the whole hour.

As I studied solution-based therapy, I decided to try out this new approach on them. They came into my office chomping at the bit, each wanting to be first to tell me who did what.

But I spoke first. "I know you have a specific argument you want to talk about, but before we do, I thought it would be good for me to hear about what has gone well for you over the last couple of months."

They both thought for a moment, and then the wife said, "We had been doing really well. We did exactly what you told us. We were talking and dating like we used to when we were first married. I felt like things were good again, but then this weekend it all fell apart."

She started to tell me what had gone wrong that weekend, but I stopped her by saying, "We'll get to that later. Tell me more about what your husband was doing to make you feel good about the relationship."

Try to focus on what's good about the marriage. You'll find it makes a big difference in your attitudes toward your spouse.

Most of the hour was spent talking about evenings out, late night discussions, and issues that had been resolved in a positive way. They both seemed to be enjoying the conversation, smiling a lot and occasionally sharing meaningful glances. Ten minutes before the end of the session I turned to the issue that brought them to my office. I reflected, "Well, it sounds like you've been doing really well, but you just got off course this weekend. Why don't you get back to what was working for you?"

They both looked at each other and smiled. "I guess we have the tools to resolve our own problems; we just need a tune-up now and then." They agreed that the argument wasn't important and that they just needed to get back to the goals they had set earlier. They needed to continue with what had been working so well.

The session was both positive and profitable. How different the session would have been if I had started by saying, "Tell me about the fight you had this weekend."

Let's get back to Bill and Patti. They left their session with the assignment to start working on each of their new goals. As one might expect, a few things went well, but most of the week was spent with the same emotional distance that they had been experiencing for months. They came to their next session ready to talk about how things had not improved much, but (as you might have guessed) I asked them to tell me about what went *right*.

Emphasizing the positive builds momentum for continued work and change.

Bill mentioned that they had one nice date that concluded with a night of intimacy, so I decided to focus on that. I asked Patti what Bill had done right that night. I then asked Bill whether he thought he could do that again and encouraged them to keep up the good work. He still needed to make some changes in his work schedule, while Patti had to work on her ability to encourage and support Bill. But again, I chose to focus our session on the positive changes that had been accomplished. They left the session encouraged and with the perspective that they were on the right track.

Emphasizing the positive builds momentum for continued work and change.

LOOK TO THE FUTURE

While traditional methods usually focus on the past, the solution approach looks to the future. Many people are quite pessimistic, seeing a bleak future for their jobs, their marriages, and their personal development. If they could rewrite the script in a more positive light, they would be better able to set goals to help them reach that great future. I often ask couples to describe their ideal future.

During one visit Bill and Patti were at a total impasse, blaming each other for a bad week. I intervened by asking both of them to imagine five or ten years into the future. I told them the future was anything they wanted it to be. Then I asked them to share their fantasies.

Patti started. "In my ideal future, Bill's business takes off and he sells it for a big profit. Then he and I only need to work on a very limited basis so we have lots of time to travel."

"Where do you go, and what do you do?" I asked.

"Europe, tropical islands, exotic places—meeting new people, sampling the foods, and having romantic getaway weekends."

"Sounds great!" I responded. "How about you Bill?"

Bill responded with a similar fantasy. He would sell his business and have the time and money to travel. But he raised a new element. "Then I'd want to start a family—perhaps a boy and a girl. We'd have a house with a big yard and a big swing set in the back."

"Really, Bill?" Patti responded. "If we're going to have a family, we'd better start sooner than five or ten years from now. That's assuming you intend to do all of this with *me!*"

"Of course," Bill laughed. "Who else would I have children with?"

My next step was to reflect to them a very positive observation. "The good news is that you are both in each other's fantasy future. That's very good. If either one of you had said, 'I'll be sailing around the world all by myself,' then I would be very worried about your relationship. It's also significant that, for both of you, Bill's business and your hectic schedules are gone in your ideal future. That shows that the enemy is not each other; the enemy of your relationship is the job and the schedule. Now, let's start talking about how you can achieve your fantasy future."

Bill and Patti really responded to the fantasy. Patti was able to see and believe that Bill wanted to spend time with her rather than work all the time. She even heard him say that a family was in their future, which made her feel more secure. She was able to be more patient and supportive of his schedule, knowing that they were working toward this better future *together.*

In solution-based therapy, there are times when the past is discussed, but this is done in order to look at what worked in the past.

A COMMON SENSE APPROACH

In solution-based therapy, there *are* times when the past is discussed, but this is done in order to look at what *worked.* "Tell me about a time when your marriage was good, and then tell me about what was different then." This reflection can build a certain confidence: "I know I can do it because I've done it before." This is especially helpful when couples have faced a similar problem in the past and worked it out.

Milton Erikson, one of the early proponents of solution-based therapy, told a funny story from his childhood. His brothers were pushing a cow, trying to get it into the barn. They pushed and pushed, but the cow wouldn't budge. Ten-year-old Milton sat watching this for a while, and then asked his older brothers if he could give it a try. They just laughed and stepped aside. Milton walked up to the cow, took hold of its tail, and gave it one huge yank. With that, the cow ran to the barn.

The moral of the story is this: If what you're doing isn't working, try something else! That's a sterling piece of common sense; but here's a corollary: If it is working, *use it!*

When it comes to healing marriages, the same common sense applies. If there are certain methods that a couple has used to grow closer together, they should use those methods again. Whatever was working, do it more. If a strategy isn't working, try a different one.

I asked Bill and Patti, "Has your marriage always been like this?" They told me about the early days when everything was more exciting and fun. "What was different then?" I wondered.

"We talked all the time," Patti answered.

"We actually looked forward to spending time together," said Bill. "At least I did."

"Me too," Patti concurred.

I prodded a little. "How about more recently? Was there any time when you felt the same way?"

This took a little more time, but Bill was able to recall a recent weekend at the beach. "We had that old magic back again," he said.

"What was different then?" I asked.

As we talked, Bill and Patti began to see that they had the resources for a good marriage, they just had to keep doing what worked and to stop doing what wasn't working.

A woman came to me for counseling because she was married to a man who never wanted to go anywhere or do anything. She would beg and plead with him to take her out or to have some kind of social life. It never seemed to work. I decided to take a chance and encouraged her to make plans to go out on her own one night, without talking to her husband. Later that week, she got dressed up and came downstairs, ready to go out with her friends.

If a strategy isn't working, try a different one!

Predictably, her husband demanded to know where she was going and then grumbled that he wasn't included. She merely said, "Well, if you want to come next time, just speak up."

The next time she mentioned she was going out to a movie, he made sure he was ready to go too. They've been going out together regularly ever since.

Was this manipulation? I don't think so. It was a way of yanking the cow's tail; she was trying a different way of expressing her feelings. As couples bring new life to their marriages, they may have to hunt for some creative ways to express themselves and to find new ways to relate to each other, to bump themselves out of old, unsatisfactory ruts.

ACTIONS SPEAK LOUDER THAN FEELINGS

One such creative technique is the act-as-if principle. On the surface it may seem phoney or hypocritical, but it's actually a clever way of letting the will win out over emotions.

Many couples do not work on their goals or perhaps refuse to try because they don't feel like it. Maybe you've had this feeling (or this lack of feeling). The spark has died, the love has flown, there is no *oompf* to save the marriage.

So *pretend*.

Even when you don't feel like going out on a date with your spouse, act as if you do. When you're not really interested in what your spouse did today, act as if you are.

The fact is that sometimes the actions lead us to the feelings. You might find that the date is really quite enjoyable. You might find that your spouse has some interesting things to say.

Some might argue that this is deceitful behavior, inappropriate for a Christian. We would argue that this notion is very biblical. Jesus told the story of the father who asked his two sons to work in the field. One son said he would but didn't. The other refused but ultimately did what the father requested. "Which one obeyed his father?" Jesus asked. The one who did the work even though he said he wouldn't.

Our feelings will not always lead us to enthusiastically do the right thing. Sometimes we have to decide to do it simply because it's the right thing to do.

The Bible exhorts husbands to love their wives and wives to respect their husbands. This becomes a problem when wives are not very lovable and husbands are not very respectable. But the biblical command is not an if-then proposition: "If your wife is acting lovable, then love her." When husbands don't feel like loving and wives don't feel like respecting, that is when they need to *act as if* they do. This may be one of the hardest things a person has to do, but we have seen it work again and again. When a person acts in a specific way, God will honor the efforts, and in time the appropriate feelings will follow.

Our feelings will not always lead us to enthusiastically do the right thing. Sometimes we have to do it simply because it's the right thing to do.

I asked Patti to show interest in Bill's job as one of her goals. Yet Patti confided that she resented Bill's job. She didn't know how she could seem pleasantly interested.

"How do you act when you're in a good mood and Bill comes home early?" I asked her. "How do you act when you're upset and Bill comes home late? The next time he comes home late, act the same way as when he comes home early, and see what happens."

Patti later reported that she tried this. Bill worked late one night, but Patti greeted him in a kind and understanding way. She acted as if he were early, and what would have been a cold evening turned out pretty well.

WHERE TO GO FROM HERE

You may be trying to keep your marriage together, more than together — alive, exciting, loving. Whether you've gone to counseling already, or have just begun to assemble a library of self-help books, watch out for the methods that just keep rehashing the old problems. If you find yourself spending all your time researching the ancient history of your life and no time learning how to talk with your spouse, there's something wrong. Psychological excavation has some value, but its value is limited. You need a new approach.

In solution-based therapy, you will find principles that can jolt you out of the doldrums. As you apply the principles explained in this book, you will discover the marriage-saving tools you already have. And as you focus on the positive, on the future, on what works, you'll sharpen those tools and use them to rebuild your relationship.

SOLUTION WORKSHOP THREE

GOAL: Begin evaluating your marriage in terms of solutions.

1. What was the first thing that attracted you to your spouse? What did you appreciate most about your spouse as you got to know him or her?

2. Imagine that after you go to bed tonight God does a miracle in your life. He heals your marriage. He makes it the kind of marriage that you both are looking for and that is honoring to Him. When you wake up in the morning, what would be different, and how would you know that the miracle had happened? How would *you* be different?

3. What does your fantasy future look like? What would you like your life to be like in five years? In ten years? What will it take for you to get there?

▼ ▼

CHAPTER FOUR

Making Your Marriage a Place of Safety

Gail and Kevin came to my* office hurt and angry at each other. Kevin called to set up the appointment because on their anniversary, Gail told Kevin she wasn't sure she wanted to be married to him. She left that day and moved in with her parents.

In my office, Gail described her expectations of what she wanted from marriage to Kevin—that he would meet her needs for affection; that they would enjoy long talks about each other's day; that they would enjoy gardening together; and most importantly, that he would be industrious, tackling chores around the home diligently.

When he did not meet those expectations, she felt deprived and disappointed. In response, she repeatedly reminded him of her expectations (and her disappointment in him), which only seemed to make matters worse. Kevin lapsed into long periods of silence, during which her attempts at affection or communication were repulsed.

Kevin also had expectations for marriage. He worked at a hard, physical job and enjoyed relaxing at home. He wanted affection, affirmation, and companionship from Gail. He expected Gail to affirm his hard work ethic and role as provider,

---

*All first person pronouns in this chapter refer to Tom Bartlett.

appreciating the material goods that he was able to give. When Gail didn't give him the nurturing he expected but instead placed further demands and criticism on him, he withdrew, kept quiet, and found ways to avoid the household duties Gail wanted done.

A cycle of hurt, blame, and anger was in full swing. Each perceived the other as an enemy, out to hurt, criticize, and attack.

How could this have happened? When Kevin and Gail first met, being with each other felt like the most secure place in the world—and now it had become a source of the greatest pain. Both partners felt insecure with the person they had vowed to cherish and trust. The one they had become most vulnerable with knew exactly where to attack. Over the years, as the relationship moved from idealistic oneness of romance to the reality of the power struggle, fear and defensiveness began to characterize their relationship.

The one they had become most vulnerable with knew exactly where to attack.

How had fear and conflict come to replace the security and oneness of romance? Both were now at a place where the person they had trusted and cared for most was the very person with whom they experienced the most hurt. Each was beginning to see the other as the enemy—"I must do whatever I can to protect myself from him or I will get hurt again." Unspoken—and maybe even unthought—but certainly felt at a subconscious level were the sensations "She means to hurt me," "He's trying to cause me pain," "She's unsafe," "He's not to be trusted."

Safety is a crucial, if not *the* most crucial, issue in marriage. It is foundational to any solution-based efforts to restore a marriage. The most clever solutions will fail if the partners do not feel safe enough to try them. Job one is to reestablish safety in your marriage.

Your brain can perform some amazing feats, but it also has a built-in need for safety. From childhood, we evaluate the world around us, constantly seeking to avoid stress or discomfort and instead to seek out comfort or pleasure. In virtually every situation, we ask, "Is this safe?"

When you are invited to a party where you may not know many people . . .

When you have to ask the boss for a day off . . .

When you're driving through a strange town and don't know where you are . . .

These are just some of the everyday situations where we find ourselves evaluating the degree of safety or threat. At a subconscious level we *need* to feel secure. We lash out or withdraw in various ways when we don't. Safety usually only becomes a conscious concern when people are dealing with physical or emotional abuse.

If we treat our spouses the way we would like to be treated, we will avoid many of the selfish actions that bring a sense of threat to our marriages.

In marriage, the need for safety provides fuel for the ongoing power struggle. When a conflict arises, both partners react to more than just the conflict itself. Each one fears that the other may hurt, ridicule, reject, or abandon—so both spouses react at a gut level (in ways they may not understand). Each gut-level reaction provokes more fear in the other partner, who responds in kind—and the conflict escalates. In order to successfully negotiate the power struggle, partners *must* establish safety in the relationship. They must find ways to assure each other that they mean no harm—and then live up to that assurance. Only then can healing begin.

The Golden Rule applies: "Do to others what you would have them do to you" (Matthew 7:12). If we treat our spouses the way we would like to be treated, not only will we express kindness and love, we will avoid many of the selfish actions that bring a sense of threat to our marriages. "Honor one another above yourselves," writes Paul (Romans 12:10), and a few verses later, "If it is possible, as far as it depends on you, live at peace with everyone" (12:18).

Of course, Paul is writing to the whole church, but his exhortations apply even more strongly to husbands and wives. Basic Christian love, expressed consistently, can do a great deal to make a marriage a safe haven. But the sober voice of realism is heard in the apostle's use of the phrase "if it is possible." Creating and maintaining safety in a relationship isn't as easy as it might seem.

WHY IS SAFETY AN ISSUE?

WE HAVE BEEN PROGRAMMED!

As human beings, we are hard wired for survival. In order for us to survive, God created us with a built-in civil defense system that scans the horizon for threat and then provides various plans of action if a danger blip shows up on the screen. If we did not have this programming, humanity would have vanished from the face of the earth long ago. While this is wonderful for avoiding death, it doesn't always help us form intimate, safe relationships. Scientists have come to describe this programming as the *fight-or-flight* response to threat.

In situations where escape is not available and the threat is too powerful to fight, the basic human response is to freeze or to submit.

Think back to the last time you were terribly frightened. You most likely experienced a rush of adrenaline accompanied by either an impulse to attack the source of the threat or an impulse to "leap out of your skin" and escape the frightful situation. In situations where escape is not available and the threat is too powerful to fight, the basic human response is to freeze or to submit.

When conflict occurs in marriage, there is fear. It may or may not be a fear of physical danger, but it is fear nonetheless — a threat of being emotionally wounded, of losing one's mate, of our own weaknesses being exposed. In other words, you fight because you don't feel safe — it's human instinct.

Larry Hof at the Marriage Council of Philadelphia describes and illustrates the fight-or-flight principle. He states that negative conflict occurs because of fear and the wish behind the fear—a wish to be close, intimate, accepted. The fear is that you won't meet my needs and that you will hurt me. In order for you not to hurt me, I must have my defenses engaged, which leads to negative conflict. The result of our conflict confirms my fear, and the stage is set for the cycle to start over again.

wish/fear/defense/conflict/defense/fear/wish[1]

When an animal feels threatened, it howls or hisses, and may attack. It is perfectly understandable for the creature to do this—that's just in its nature. And what do you do when your pet becomes defensive? You lessen the threat. You put your arm down, kneel to the animal's level, speak in calming tones. "It's all right, Pookie. I won't hurt you."

Human instinct is very similar, and we see it often in marriage. The solution is also similar. When you and your spouse start barking at each other, you must lessen the threat. You must work to *create* safety.

FAULTY FOUNDATIONS

Another reason we seek safety in marriage goes back to our families of origin. Growing up, all of us experienced emotional hurts or unmet needs, in varying degrees. Some endured physical, sexual, or emotional abuse, while others have grown up in single-parent homes. Some had dads who were always off on business trips, while others had moms who were emotionally unavailable due to

Even if you haven't faced physical abuse, you still learned to fear emotional wounding.

life stressors or emotional problems. Even in the best of homes, parents cannot always meet a child's legitimate needs, the result is that one of the most basic childhood emotions is *disappointment.* We get hurt.

Childhood wounds, no matter how minor or how deep, make up much of how we see ourselves (and how we believe others see us). Our early hurts teach us to protect ourselves, to guard our fragile egos, to shield our timid loves, to defend against everyday pains. Even if you haven't faced physical abuse, you still learned to fear *emotional* wounding.

The defenses that allowed us to survive the disappointments of childhood become the defenses in our marriages that lead to the negative conflict cycle.

Barb and Steve had been married for twenty years and were contemplating separation and divorce. As they met with me, it became clear very quickly that they each felt very wounded and attacked by the other. Barb grew up in a family where her feelings were discounted. Her father was uncommunicative and, when angry, would withdraw from her and not communicate.

Steve grew up in a family with high expectations. There was always something he could have done better. He developed a high need for affirmation, which always seemed to elude him.

When they met, it seemed to be a perfect match. She found someone who was emotional, involved, and wanted to take care of her—fulfilling her desire for attention. He found someone who looked up to him and thought everything he did was wonderful—fulfilling his need for affirmation.

After they were married, though, she noticed that he often became moody, quiet, and withdrawn. The same fear of abandonment from childhood enveloped her, and she would express anger at his withdrawal. Steve felt criticized and unaffirmed. Rather than risk further hurt, he avoided her and the cycle continued.

By the time they came to my office, Steve felt as though he were being attacked by a dog. She thought he was running away from her and shutting her out. Childhood issues were being replayed in their marriage.

While the solution approach does focus on the future rather than the past, it does not ignore the past. In fact, past issues must be recognized in order to analyze the current sense of safety. Barb began to see her father's withdrawal in Steve, and she was afraid Steve would become unavailable to her as well. When she confronted Steve about this behavior, he felt attacked—bringing up old fears of failing to meet his family's high standards. Why did Barb and Steve feel unsafe? The answer is in the past.

The key to the solution approach is this: You cannot undo the pain of the past, but you *can* keep it from hurting your future. Barb and Steve needed to draw a line in the sand and say, "That was then; this is now. You are not my father, you are not my mother. We can start a new system here that's safe for both of us."

SAFETY THROUGH THE STAGES OF MARRIAGE

As we said, we enter marriage with expectations. We expect our mates to meet our needs, to make us whole. We expect the other person to make us feel wonderful and happy.[2] Especially if we grew up in an unsafe environment, we expect we will finally find safety in marriage. "Here is the person I can't live without, the person I trust with my life," we reason, and so we begin to lower our defenses.

As a counselor I often hear couples in this stage say, "I've told this person things I've never told anyone else." As a sense of trust develops, we are willing to risk more—willing to be more vulnerable and share more of ourselves, our hurts, and our needs, with our spouse. Of course, the same thing is happening with our spouse. They have needs, too.

"Hey, wait a minute! I thought you were supposed to meet *my* needs!"

"I'm tired of meeting your needs. What about *mine?*"

In this power struggle, both partners start to take more than they give. It becomes a zero-sum game: my attention to *your* needs distracts us both from meeting *my* needs. Now when I express fear, sadness, or hurt, my spouse may ignore my feelings—or worse yet, attack me for feeling the way I do. Similarly, I may attack my spouse in order to focus on my needs. Harville Hendrix gave this explanation: "As conditions deteriorate, we decide that the best way to force our partners to satisfy our needs is to be unpleasant and irritable, just as we were in the cradle."³ In such a combat situation, my civil defense system reaches red alert—not to survive a physical threat, but to defend against the annihilation of my ego—my personhood.

As we saw in the example of Barb and Steve, marriage in the stage of energized conflict becomes a process of refortifying the old defenses put up in childhood. It isn't hard to recognize that a built-in survival response to fear is fight or flight. Therefore, when one spouse fears that the other will bring harm or wounding again, he or she begins to rely on the old response of either withdrawing or attacking (the best defense is a good offense).

The curious thing about the process is that it involves two people who care about each other, but are afraid of being hurt. But they keep hurting each other because they think that will keep them from getting hurt. As they weary of the conflict, they enter the stalemate stage, where they find a kind of safety in their Cold War.

It's like two old gunfighters pointing their weapons at each other, fingers on the triggers in a tense standoff. As they realize that they both are horribly vulnerable, they begin to think about backing out of the situation but neither wants to be the first to lower his gun. They have two choices: Stand there forever, at the ready, doomed to die of old age; or one of them could make the first move to begin to lower the gun slowly and step back. Often that is the stage at which people seek counseling. They are in a classic gunfighters' standoff, both afraid to lower the gun lest the other blow them away.

WHAT DOES SAFETY LOOK LIKE?

When people come to us for counseling, they're usually not thinking about safety. They want to rekindle the old spark. They want to live together without driving each other crazy. They want to stop having those awful fights.

But safety is the solution they seek.

Most of us, if we take a moment to think, are looking for the knowledge that we are accepted and loved unconditionally, that we will still be loved even though we are flawed. Most of us are well aware of our own flaws, but we don't want to be reminded of them constantly. We need to know that we have value in our spouse's eyes.

We've learned a few things about safety from group therapy. During the first meeting of a support group, it's tough to get people to speak up. People hunch over in their chairs, guarding their private space, answering questions a few syllables at a time. What are they afraid of? The group! These are strangers who might criticize anything they say.

Over time, however, group members begin to open up. As each one shares his or her story, they develop a kind of intimacy. They feel more comfortable with one another, safer. They know their comments will be met with respect and empathy.

So when a marriage is unsafe, what are the partners really most afraid of?

At some level, most fear that their *self-worth* will be threatened. This may be tied to looks, accomplishments, habits, or ideas—but it comes down to personal value. Will their spouse affirm them or tear them down?

People also fear that their *communication* will be misunderstood, ridiculed, or unheard. This fear, too, relates to self-worth, so a stranglehold on communication can choke a relationship. Will their spouse listen to what they say and respond with respect?

Some fear that their *actions* will be unsupported, belittled, or sabotaged. Whether it's fixing the water heater or running for office, people put themselves on the line when they try new things. An uncooperative spouse can quash the best-laid plans. Will their partner appreciate their efforts and help them out?

Others fear that their *feelings* will be discounted. People don't always understand their emotions, but emotions affect everything they do. If feelings cannot be expressed openly, a relationship stagnates. Will their spouse make an effort to understand how they feel?

With all the talk of gender differences these days (see chapter 5), we're tempted to say that men deal more with the action issues and women more with feelings, but that isn't really the case. It is true that men tend to define themselves by what they do and that women tend to place more value in emotions, but in marriage these values can flip flop. That is, a wife may feel great pressure in, say, fixing a water heater because she wants to prove herself valuable to her husband. A husband may be insecure sharing his feelings because it's not his turf. He may feel something strongly but not know how to express it, and thus fear the condescension of his emotion-oriented wife.

What does safety look like? How do safe marriages guard the self-worth, communication, actions, and feelings of both partners? Think about the strong marriages you've seen. What factors did you see?

It seems to start with *respect*. Both partners operate from a basic ground rule: "You are important." That doesn't mean that there is always agreement, but both partners generally take time to listen, understand, and respond—because they consider their spouse worth it.

There's also a *win-win spirit*. If one spouse wins at the other's expense, there's no victory. Safe marriages have a sense of common fortune. In arguments, they seek solutions they both can live with. No one's keeping score.

We also find strong *involvement* in safe marriages. The partners have a way of *being there* for each other. The husband puts down the paper when his wife starts talking (though she may ask first whether it's a good time to talk). In fact, the husband is usually so *present* for his wife when they're together that she doesn't mind him taking time alone when he needs it. When she struggles with her feelings, he is there with a hug. When he feels threatened at work, she offers a supportive compliment. Each is tuned in to the other's needs.

Finally, we see *support* as a crucial factor in safe marriages. Both partners go out of their way to help the other. The husband gladly types his wife's master's thesis. She patiently reschedules the family vacation when her husband learns he has to work. This support is especially noticeable when a crisis arises—one spouse loses a job, there's a busy time at work, or there are emotionally wrenching problems with parents or children. When one partner's physical or emotional strength is sapped, the other fills the gap.

AM I SAFE?

On a scale of 1 to 10, with 10 being "perfectly safe" and 1 being "not safe at all," indicate how safe you feel in your marriage.

I feel valued and assured of *worth*.

    1   2   3   4   5   6   7   8   9   10

I feel that what I *say* is important to my spouse.

    1   2   3   4   5   6   7   8   9   10

The things that I *do* in our relationship are valued.

    1   2   3   4   5   6   7   8   9   10

My *feelings* are validated.

    1   2   3   4   5   6   7   8   9   10

I feel *respected* in our relationship.

    1   2   3   4   5   6   7   8   9   10

When problems arise, my spouse will *assume the best* about me.

    1   2   3   4   5   6   7   8   9   10

I know that my spouse will always *be there* for me.

    1   2   3   4   5   6   7   8   9   10

I feel *supported* in what I do and say.

    1   2   3   4   5   6   7   8   9   10

WHAT'S THE SOLUTION?

It's a nice picture, isn't it? The safe marriage looks ideal, but how do you ever get there?

1. Decide to disarm. Think back to the two gunfighters. The only way they both walk away unharmed is if one (or maybe even both simultaneously) determines to risk putting down the gun.

If you want to feel safe in your marriage, you must be a source of safety for your spouse. Most of us would have no difficulty identifying some threats we feel from our spouse, yet we might be surprised to hear the many ways we make our spouse feel unsafe. The first step toward safety is to commit *yourself* to be safer for your spouse. It is an individual responsibility to *be* a safe person.

You cannot work on the solutions you need for a healthy marriage unless you know that your spouse is not poised to harm you at the first opportunity—and your spouse needs to know the same about you.

When you commit to make the relationship safe for your spouse and your spouse does the same for you, you are beginning the journey toward unconditional acceptance that most of us wish for. When your marriage is safe, you can talk about your feelings and your weaknesses without the fear of abandonment or rejection. Only then can you reveal your true hurts to each other so that healing can begin.

2. Sign on the dotted line. Have you decided to make your marriage safer? Then ask your spouse to join you in the commitment and put it in writing.

The Safety Contract is one vital technique we use in marital therapy. Most couples agree that they do not intend to hurt each other, but sometimes they just can't help it. The Safety Contract invites both parties to affirm their intentions of safety. Within the contract, both admit that they often act defensively and may hurt the other without meaning to, and commit to changing their unsafe behaviors.

The Safety Contract allows both partners to give each other the benefit of the doubt. When one spouse says or does something hurtful, the other can see that he or she is not the enemy, but just a fallible human being. One spouse may slip back into defensiveness, but the other does not need to respond in kind. If one spouse gives the other the benefit of the doubt, assuming that he or she really wants to do things right, they can get the relationship back on track before too long. (There's a safety contract at the end of this chapter for you and your spouse to complete.)

3. Find a safe place to talk. The Safety Contract is just the beginning—you two have a lot to talk about. The process of restoring safety requires a lot of "You know, I don't like it when you do that," and "Here's what you do to make me feel unsafe."

Ironically, this part of the process can be extremely threatening. You're like minesweepers, trying to make the terrain safe by finding the explosives and disarming them—but it's very dangerous work. Therefore, you need to take extra precautions to ensure safety during this process.

Counseling may be the safest option at this point. A psychologist's office ethically and legally has been designated as a place where people can share their innermost thoughts and feelings without the fear of ridicule or exposure. That private, confidential office means safety—safety to share and safety to heal. It may also help to have the counselor as a sort of referee, enforcing your own ground rules.

But you can also create a safe haven in your home. Set apart a room or corner of your home as the place where you'll do your toughest negotiations and designate other areas (such as the bedroom) as demilitarized zones.

Set aside certain times when you will discuss these issues, but then relax and enjoy each other the rest of the time. Learn to table some discussions—putting them off for later, better times—and call a timeout when talks start to get out of hand.

4. Learn from the past. Take some time to look at a recent conflict or series of conflicts which caused you to feel hurt or angry with your spouse. Step away from it and analyze. Why did you say this? Why did your spouse do that? What did you say or do that may have made you appear unsafe in your spouse's eyes?

5. Put it in writing. Like the gunfighter in our illustration, you might consider making the first gesture toward safety by lowering the gun. Write your spouse a note, indicating that you want to be a safer partner. Ask your spouse to write down some of the things you do that make him or her feel unsafe. Also ask what behaviors would make your spouse feel safer.

SAMPLE LETTER TO SPOUSE

I know that recently it seems as though we have had some conflict or trouble being happy with each other. I want you to know that I care a great deal about you and our marriage. I don't really know all the things that we need to do, but I would like us to begin to make things better. I would like to become someone with whom you feel safe and happy. I am sure there are things that I have done or continue to do that have caused you to feel unsafe around me.

I want to hear what you have to say and take steps to make our marriage safer. In order to do that, I would like you to take time to think about this and write down some of the things that I do in either word or action that make our marriage not as safe as it could be. While some of these things may be difficult for me to read, I promise I will thoughtfully consider them and work to make our marriage safer.

6. Ask God to open your heart and mind. I was recently speaking to a group about the issue of safety, and in particular, giving your spouse the benefit of the doubt. One woman in the group raised her hand, and with tears in her eyes she asked, "What do you do when your spirits are so closed and you both have been so wounded by the other person that you can no longer trust or open yourself up to your spouse?"

I paused for a while, knowing the pain she must be in. I see this type of relationship often and know there are no easy answers. In fact there *is* no answer to this problem. It would take a miracle at this point to undo the damage done by years of verbal, emotional, or even physical abuse. So that is what I told her. "It would take a miracle. Therefore, you and your husband need to pray that God would open your hearts and minds to one another."

I don't want to be accused of applying a spiritual Band-Aid, but I know of no other way to open a heart once it has been completely shut. Even when you do something nice or helpful for your spouse, it can be misinterpreted as having a selfish motive. We must call upon the healing power of the Holy Spirit to begin a work in our hearts and minds.

LISTENING TO THE VOICE OF REALITY

Safety. It's a nice idea. But does it work?

If you just start to offer safety to your spouse, will he or she immediately respond in kind and ride off with you into the sunset of eternal bliss? Of course!

You're not buying that, are you? Good.

The solution approach is practical and realistic. It does no good to dream of instant solutions for problems that took years to develop. Chances are, you've been in a destructive spiral of withdrawal and attack, reopening old wounds and inflicting new ones. You are now trying to slow that spiral down, to stop it, and to begin healing. As your marriage becomes a sanctuary of safety, you can begin to build intimacy. "If it's safe, I can trust you enough to let you get closer."

But it won't happen overnight.

Remember the image of the gunfighters. If you begin lowering your gun, what happens? You don't know. Maybe you'll get shot to pieces. Maybe your spouse will stay there, armed and dangerous. Maybe it will take a long time before you see any progress.

The two of you have built up a series of expectations about each other. You know what your spouse is going to say before he or she speaks—and you are usually ready to respond before any words are spoken. You could probably carry on most of your marital arguments by yourself. Maybe you do. You're like two star tennis players playing each other for the hundredth time. You know each other's game. You play the same strokes again and again. Who's going to win this time?

In a way, it's a dance, and you both know the steps. You may not like the dance, but you don't seem to be able to stop. The commitment to creating safety will change the dance steps but you have to expect to get your toes stepped on in the process. You may flinch or say "ouch," but your commitment to safety means you'll continue to practice the new steps.

If both you and your spouse have committed to make the marriage safer, the dance can change at a surprising rate. If you're the only one committed to safety, you can still work toward changing the dance, it just may take a little longer to see progress.

Remember that you are on a pathway, a journey. You came through the gilded halls of *infatuation* and are dancing through the swamps of the *negotiation*. Eventually, though, you may reach the level ground of *mature love*. You will be amazed what starts to happen when you commit to creating safety for your spouse. It is a process that heals your relationship and some of your own wounds and disappointments in the process. In the next few chapters we will provide you with communication tools and insights that will help you find some solutions, building strength and stability upon the foundation of safety.

SOLUTION WORKSHOP FOUR

GOAL: Create safety in your relationship.

1. Look back at the "Am I Safe?" Test that you took (page 85). In which areas are you feeling fairly safe, say at least above a 5? In which areas do you sense your relationship could use some improvement, a 5 or below?

2. Using solution-based techniques (i.e., future focus, not arguing the past), what behaviors could your spouse exhibit that would

help you feel safer in each of the problem areas? Write down those behaviors so that he or she can practice them.

For the Wife—Behavior to Improve

Area 1:

Area 2:

Area 3:

Area 4:

For the Husband—Behavior to Improve

Area 1:

Area 2:

Area 3:

Area 4:

3. Don't do any more than four problem areas or your spouse will feel overwhelmed, perhaps even unsafe. Work on the areas listed here for four to six months, check for improvement, and then if there are more areas to improve, add a few more.

Exercise One: Safety Contract
   ▼ Read the Safety Contract on the next page carefully.
   ▼ Make two copies of the blank contract. (Limited permission is granted to photocopy this contract for use by you and your

spouse in conjunction with your study of *The Marriage Mender*. No pages in any other part of this book may be copied, nor may this contract be copied for any other reason.)

▼ Talk about any issues involved in agreeing to the contract.

▼ Set up a time to sign the contract together and commit yourselves to making the marriage safe.

▼ After signing the contract, each of you should keep a copy of the contract to remind you of your pledge.

Safety Contract

1. By word or action, I do not intend to hurt you.

2. Believing the same of you, I do recognize that because we are both fallible human beings, we may hurt each other inadvertently or out of defensiveness.

3. Therefore, I will strive to give you the benefit of the doubt, and if I am hurt by your word or action, I will not view it as intentional but will attempt to communicate my hurt to you.

4. When you communicate your hurt from my word or action, I will acknowledge your feelings and will talk with you about ways to prevent a reoccurrence in the future.

5. I know that this will take work and courage, but I also know that we both want the same goal of safety and acceptance from each other.

I, _____, pledge to work to become a
       name
person with whom you, _____, feel safe.
            spouse's name

Date: Signed:

Exercise Two: Learn from the Past

Think about some incident or argument you had recently that threatened, even in a small way, the safety of your marriage. As you talk together about it, try to remember the exact words that were said. Write a short script of the incident, as if you were writing a play. (An example follows.)

Then go back through it, line by line, asking each other, "Why did you say that? What were you feeling? How did you interpret what I said?" To one side, write notes about the subtext of the dialogue.

EXAMPLE

SCRIPT	NOTES
SHE: Honey, we need to talk about this weekend.	*She wants to arrange a social event.*
HE: (watching TV) Wait a minute! The game's almost over.	*Big game. He's been looking forward to it.*
SHE: It's just a game. We need to make plans so I can call Julie.	*She feels shut out.*
HE: We can do it later.	*He feels she doesn't care about what he likes.*
SHE: But Julie needs to know so she can get a sitter.	*She's trying to be kind to Julie.*
HE: Quit bothering me! We'll talk about it later.	*He doesn't know how hard it is to get a sitter. He can't focus on the game; it makes him mad.*
SHE: Is that all I am? A bother? (leaves in tears)	*She feels unimportant.*

Exercise Three: Letter to Spouse

Reread the sample letter on page 88 and write something similar, expressing your own feelings about safety to your spouse.

▼

PART TWO

Solution-Based Approaches to Communication Problems

▼ ▼

CHAPTER FIVE

Identifying Your Communication Styles

A spaceship lands on the White House lawn. Aliens step out, tall and thin, with a few too many eyes. We don't expect them to speak our language, so we send in our best linguists and they crack the code. Soon we are communicating pretty well with these extraterrestrials.

Oh, there are a few words we will never understand, since they have to do with features of their home planet. And they seem to have trouble with some of our language, especially the lyrics to our pop tunes of the fifties. But, over time, we learn to appreciate what these aliens have to offer. For instance, they have mastered microwave technology to the point where they can beam objects to different locations, but they were never very good with popcorn until they learned our Redenbacher secrets.

Now back to earth. The point is, you should consider your spouse an alien. Maybe you already do!

Major mistakes are made when a wife expects her husband to talk and think just as she does, or when a husband is peeved that his wife isn't like him. We are different beings with different ways. To preserve safety in marriage and to discover solutions to our marital struggles, we must understand that we're different.

When the aliens land on the White House lawn, some citizens get spooked. They fear this invasion from space, assuming that the extraterrestrials are hostile. People always tend to fear the unknown, the different—even in marriages.

Since your spouse is not using your language or your methods to conduct his or her half of the relationship, you may feel insecure. Safety requires understanding and accepting those differences. Solutions are found in appreciation of differences.

TALKING IT OVER

"We need to talk."

Imagine that your spouse comes to you with that phrase. How do you respond? Does that strike terror in your heart? Or are you happy for the chance to engage in meaningful conversation? Or is the whole scene absurd because your spouse would never say those words?

Your answer may depend on your gender.

If you are a man, chances are that talking does not come easy for you—especially talking about relationships. (There are plenty of men who can talk endlessly about baseball or politics but who clam up when asked to express their feelings.)

If you are a woman, you may welcome the opportunity to discuss your relationship, though it may be surprising to hear your husband instigate the discussion.

As this simple example shows, the most significant gender differences occur in styles of communication. Women usually feel threatened in a relationship by a lack of verbal communication. They feel they are losing touch. Men, on the other hand, often feel threatened by intimate conversation about the relationship. They may fear that they will have to discuss their feelings, something they usually don't do very well.

You should consider your spouse an alien. Maybe you already do!

A DISCLAIMER

Notice the words *may*, *often*, and *usually*. Certain characteristics may be true of 70 to 80 percent of men or women, but you may be in the other 20 or 30 percent. There are always exceptions. It would be false to say, "Men always do this; women are always like that." But research shows men *tend to* do such-and-such more than women do, or vice versa.

So we're saying that most women *tend to* talk about emotions and relationships more than most men do. We can theorize about women's biological role as nurturer and cultural role as caretaker of family life.

Admittedly, we need to be careful with this theory, too. Are the differences between men and women biological or cultural? Are men and women born with differences, or have we learned them? The verdict is still pending, though there have been fascinating findings about the makeup of men's and women's brains. The answer, as we go through our list of male-female differences, is probably, "Both." We have biological differences *and* cultural differences.

We also need to be careful about passing judgment. After centuries of men complaining about the oddities of women (remember "Why Can't a Woman Be More Like a Man?" from *My Fair Lady?*) the last decade has seen a rise of male bashing. Both are inappropriate. Men's differences do not make them better or worse than women—just different. The same is true for women. Once we accept that differences do exist and that these aren't good or bad—just different—we can move forward to real communication.

And that's our aim: communication. As you seek solutions to your marital struggles, you need to know that men and women essentially speak different languages. Any effective solution will include some translation work.

What she says: "We need to talk."

What he thinks she means: "You have done something to offend me."

What she probably really means: "I need some affirmation or support from you."

If he says they need to talk, he means: "We need to make plans for Saturday night."

WEIRD SCIENCE

Using new technologies called Functional Magnetic Residence Imaging (FMRI) and Positron Emission Tomography (PET), researchers at the University of Pennsylvania looked at the differences in brain activity between men and women.[1] Researchers found that men showed more activity in the brain region that controls *emotions linked to action*, especially aggression, while women showed more activity in the region that controls *complex expression of emotion*.

They also looked at the issue of how well men and women are able to read emotion on people's faces. They found that both men and women performed extremely well at judging expressions denoting happiness, but when it came to picking out facial expressions indicating sadness, there was a fascinating distinction. Women did very well identifying sadness on pictures of both men and women. On the other hand, men were able to judge male expressions of sadness as well as the women did but were much less accurate in judging sadness expressed by women. Even when women and men showed the same accuracy, the researchers found that women's brains did not have to work as hard as men's to accomplish the task.

Men do not have the same ability to read people that women have, especially when there is some empathy required.

So when men say, "Sorry, I didn't notice," maybe that's not just an excuse. It may be a genuine difference in brain function. Apparently, men do not have the same ability to read people that women have, especially when there is some empathy required. The lesson for women might be: "Yes, you really do have to spell it out for them." Generally, men will not pick up on the same subtle clues.

Imagine two hunters traipsing through a dense jungle. One is a skilled tracker. She knows how to read the clues in the vegetation—the wild animal went that-a-way. The other, knowing nothing about jungles, is scared to death. Every crackling twig, every hoot from some harmless bird is a cause for terror since he doesn't know the terrain.

Such is the difference between the typical woman and the typical man, according to this research—except the terrain is *conversation*, especially emotional conversation. Most men don't read the clues as well as women do, so they feel less secure. Let a man *do* something, and he's back in familiar territory. Let him talk about what he's doing, and he's still fine. But he begins to feel unsafe when the conversation slides onto emotional turf.

> *In marriage two people are coming from two different cultures, attempting to speak and communicate in a shared language.*

EMOTIONS AND SAFETY

Another study at Yale University gave men and women a rhyming task. The men who were tested utilized only the left side of the brain, which is associated with verbal reasoning. Women, on the other hand, were found to use both left and right sides of the brain, indicating that they drew on feeling as well as reason. The implication of this research is that it may validate what many people have observed about men and women and relationships—that men tend to be more focused on reasoning, fixing, or dealing with the bottom line in communication, often ignoring the emotional elements or finding them irrelevant to resolving the problem. On the other hand, women may view the problem and its resolution as inseparable from the feelings associated with it.[2]

Let's get back to those hunters in the jungle. The skilled tracker suddenly loses the trail of the wild beast. With no clue about the creature's location, now she is terrified. Maybe it doubled back and is stalking them. Maybe it is hiding in the undergrowth. The uncertainty makes her feel very unsafe.

So it is in many relationships when a man does not communicate his emotions. The woman, skilled at reading clues, sees absolutely nothing, and she worries that the relationship is in danger. Since her brain ties emotion together with every other function, she fears the worst when she gets no emotional interaction from her husband.

So the very thing that assures her of safety—emotional conversation—tends to threaten him. And when he is safely ensconced in his world of nonemotional discourse, she feels unsafe.

Can such a couple ever find a solution to their communication problems? Is there a way out of this catch-22? Sure, but it takes some understanding and risk taking on both sides.

The man must take the risk of communicating his emotions, and the woman must learn to provide a safe environment for him to do so. She must avoid the temptation to finish his sentences, to usurp his feelings, to react too quickly or strongly—whether her reaction is positive or negative.

Men have a way of evaluating a task and saying to themselves, "If I can't excel at something, I don't want to do it at all," and they apply this to expressing emotions, too. Since it's generally female turf, men can get frustrated with their inability to express emotions. To save face, they often discount the importance of emotional discourse. "Now don't get all emotional, dear." Men often divorce facts from feelings, prizing facts much more. Of course, this can make women feel silly for being more emotional. All of this self-talk contributes to the stalemate.

Every case is different, but here are some general solutions for husbands and wives.

Husbands. Emotions are important, and you hurt yourself when you wall them off. Men who learn to talk about their feelings—even in a halting way—make better husbands. Sure, it's a risk to do something you're not good at, but it's worth the effort.

You need to affirm the importance of emotions both in your wife and in yourself. When your wife is expressing her emotions, don't discount them. And don't try to fix everything. Let her feel what she's feeling. Hug her. Tell her you love her. She needs to know that her feelings are respected. And to know that you have to *tell* her.

When you have strong feelings you need to express, take a

chance and share them with your wife. It's risky to be honest about feelings you don't fully understand, to *not* have all the answers for a change, to let your wife teach you some things about emotions.

Wives. You need to do what you can to lessen the risk for your husband. Allow your husband to struggle with emotional expression, understanding that he will probably not open up emotionally as much as you'd like.

Control is important for most men, especially self-control. That's why emotions are such scary territory. As a man sees it, expressing his feelings is like hiking down a steep hill— one bad step and you take a tumble. Many women have mastered the tumble; they know the value of a good cry. But most men will tread on their feelings carefully, step by step, maintaining control.

> *The solution is not to adopt the same emotional style but to understand, accept, and appreciate the differences.*

So, in emotional conversation, it's crucial to let your husband maintain his self-control. Your husband's plodding self-revelation may seem like baby steps to you, but remember that he is terrified of falling down the hill. Gently urge him, but don't rush him. Use your husband-reading skills to sense the response he wants from you: a motherly hug or a brotherly punch on the shoulder. Let him set the limits of the discussion (when you're discussing *his* emotions), and let him retreat when he needs to.

When discussing your own emotions, remember that your husband probably doesn't know what to do. Strong emotion, even in someone else, can be frightening. *Tell him* how to respond to you, when to reassure you, and when to shut up and hug you.

The emotional differences between men and women are pervasive. They affect every aspect of a marriage, and they determine the structure of our conversation. The solution is not to adopt the same emotional style but to understand, accept, and appreciate the differences.

VIVE LA DIFFERENCE!

There are many other personality differences that seem to be based in gender. Let's briefly consider some of them, along with some solutions for the difficulties they create.

COOPERATION/COMPETITION

Girls tend to play in small groups or pairs, engaging in *cooperative* activities involving communication. Boys tend to play in larger groups, and much of their activity is *competitive*. Girls learn involvement while boys learn independence.

This distinction continues throughout life. Women assume cooperation where men assume competition. For example, a wife asks her husband, "Can you help me with the dishes?"

He hears a challenge and, in his mind at least, he responds, "Yes, I am capable of doing the dishes." But will he *choose* to do the dishes? And when? He may not feel like helping out at that moment.

The wife meant something like this: "I need your help and support now, because I am working alone in the kitchen. Do you care enough about me to join me here?" In a way, she is calling out for safety, the assurance of cooperation.

When he calls from the living room, "Sure, when I'm finished with the paper," what does she hear? "No, I care more about the newspaper than you. Wait your turn." It's a major putdown, threatening her sense of security in the relationship.[3]

On the literal level at which he understands the conversation, it all seemed very straightforward to him. Can you help? Yes, but I choose to help later. He is deaf to the whole drama of need and insult that she has witnessed in the very same conversation. When she storms into the living room in tears or in rage, he wonders why. Now his safety is threatened as she accuses him of sabotaging the relationship. *What did I do?* he wonders.

Approach to a solution: Both need to translate the other's language. They need to hear the real need, and express themselves more fully. Wives can use their words to build up their husbands (granting a self-esteem victory in the warfare of life).

Husbands can use their presence and participation to satisfy their wives' need for cooperation.

INCLUSIVE/EXCLUSIVE

A second area of difference between the sexes, probably based on upbringing more than biology, is that women tend to be more *inclusive* in their thought and language, while men tend to be more *exclusive*. Some have used the image of the ancient cavewomen as gatherers. Men might go off hunting for days on end, but women were back home gathering—gathering food, gathering children, gathering information for the home and community. Women tend to have a greater sense of *us*, while men think more in the sense of *me*.

MALE FOCUS	FEMALE FOCUS
I	We
I act.	We discuss.
My world is ordered around me.	Our world flows around us.
I fight for my place in the world.	We arrange ways of living together.
I exert control over others.	I seek to include others.
I seek to have my need met.	I feel good when giving to others.

A husband and wife come home from work and she asks him about his day. She is gathering information, sharing in his activities. He may be slow in relating his experiences, and she may have to dig it out of him, asking pertinent questions until she feels sufficiently well-versed in his activities. Then she waits for him to ask her about her day.

And she waits.

If he cared, he would ask. That's what she thinks.

But he is thinking: *If she wanted me to know, she would tell me.*

She wants the safety of being included in his concerns. For her, it's a basic rule of involvement. If you care, you ask about the other person. You want to know everything about what they've been doing.

But he may have been somewhat threatened by her prying questions into his day's activities, and he has no desire to do the same to her. For him, it's a basic rule of independence. If you have something you choose to tell someone else, you say it. If not, you don't. If something important occurred, you share it. If not, why bother?

When the man does feel like talking about his day, it is usually very exclusive; it's about what makes him special, unique, or important.

"I hit a home run tonight."

"I had the best sales numbers this month."

"They all loved my presentation."

▼　▼　▼

Some might consider this selfish behavior, but it's more a safety issue. Men feel safe when they feel competent. If they have proved their competence in some way, they like to trumpet that. It's their way of sharing.

Approach to a solution: Wives, do not take your husband's "don't ask; don't tell" policy personally. Overcome it by asking good questions. Start with fact questions about him and his accomplishments. Ease into open-ended questions about his feelings. But don't beat a dead horse; sometimes he just doesn't feel like talking. Schedule a future time to talk. Husbands, make it a habit to ask your wife about her life. This may not occur to you naturally, but she thrives on it—so just make a point to do it.

FEELINGS/FACTS

Yet another difference is that of *feelings* versus *facts*. We have already considered men's general difficulty with emotions. One way of compensating is to concentrate on the cold, hard facts. Men tend to focus on the facts of a story, while women usually focus on the feelings involved. When a wife shares with her husband her feelings about a problem or incident that occurred during the day, he has to translate her feelings into facts.

SHE: I feel fat.

HE: That's silly. You're not fat.

What's happening here? They are speaking two different languages. She communicates a feeling. He receives the facts about her feelings.

- ▼ Fact 1: She feels bad because she thinks she is fat.
- ▼ Fact 2: She is not fat.
- ▼ Fact 3: Her feeling is not based on reality, therefore it makes no sense.
- ▼ Solution: She should face the truth and stop feeling that way.

Men like to fix things. If a woman communicates an undesirable feeling, the man assumes she is seeking advice on how to get rid of the feeling. He tries to talk her out of her feeling by focusing on the facts. Men feel safe with facts. With facts he knows where he stands.

The man is really trying to say the right thing, comforting his wife by assuring her of the fact that she's not fat. In his way of thinking, the assurance should settle it—but the "just the facts" approach usually makes things worse. Not only does she still feel fat, now she feels stupid for feeling fat.

Women tend to share feelings to develop intimacy. The "us" gets stronger as feelings are shared. She feels safe as she connects with her husband in this moment of self-doubt. She doesn't need him to fix the problem, she wants him to share the feeling. As we have said, feelings are a woman's turf. She wants to know that her man stands with her in those feelings.

Approach to a solution: Both spouses must understand that the world is full of facts and feelings, and both are valuable.

INTUITION/INFORMATION

Men and women also gather information in different ways. As we have mentioned, women are tuned in to a *relational* frequency, so they pick up all sorts of visual and tone-of-voice signals. Men tend to gather *concrete information*—"what you see is what you get." A male-female combination should make for a great team, one complementing the other, and sometimes it does. But problems occur when men and women fail to appreciate the other's strength in the matter. Instead of feeling more secure because their wives are using their intuition to read complex situations, many men feel threatened by it. Instead of feeling more secure because their husbands' concrete thinking is balancing out their intuition, women often feel insecure because of their husbands' seeming ignorance of the things they see as what really matters.

Especially if a marriage has lasted a while, wives often assume that their husbands should read their minds. Wives can read minds — can't everybody? But husbands get frustrated because their wives will not come out and say clearly what they want.

HE: What's bothering you, hon?

SHE: You know.

HE: What do you mean? If I knew, I wouldn't have asked.

SHE: Well, if you loved me, you'd know.

HE: Let's not start this guessing game again. Just tell me what it is so I can do something about it.

SHE: Well, when you figure out what you did wrong, you come and tell me; otherwise, I have nothing more to say about this.

The man is mystified, the woman frustrated. Is she *trying* to be difficult? Can he *really* be that ignorant? Both feel threatened in this relationship because both fail to recognize their differences. Instead of accepting their tendencies and meeting in the middle, we compound the differences by expecting our mates to think just like us.

Many couples fall into a dangerous communication cycle based on their differences.

▼ She wants him to spend more time with her.
▼ So she communicates this in subtle, but indirect, ways.
▼ Thus, she thinks he should know what she wants.
▼ He doesn't spend more time with her, seeming to ignore her subtle messages.
▼ She feels he must not love her anymore since he obviously refuses to spend more time with her.

▼ She expresses anger and hurt about this.

▼ He feels ambushed, unfairly attacked, and blamed for something he had no idea he was doing.

▼ He assumes she should know by now how to ask for what she wants.

▼ He becomes bitter about her expectations of him.

This scenario can go on and on—he waits for her to ask and she waits for him to read her hints.

Approach to a solution: Break the cycle by talking about it. A wife needs to state her needs clearly, but a husband also needs to learn to read her cues. By giving each other the benefit of the doubt, they can avoid the dangerous cycle of assumptions and hurt feelings.

The solution might yield a scene something like the following example:

HE: (sensing her displeasure) What's bothering you, hon?

SHE: (stating it clearly) I feel like you don't love me as much as you used to.

HE: (accepting her feelings and probing them) Why do you feel that way?

SHE: (speaking in facts for his benefit) You work late, and when you are home you often bring work with you. We never have any time together.

HE: (giving her the benefit of the doubt) I'm sorry. With all your activities, I didn't think that was a problem.

SHE: (explaining) I just got involved in other activities because you were never home. I thought you didn't want to be with me.

HE: (reassuring) I do. I love you. But my job really piles on the work.

SHE: (negotiating, asking for what she wants) I know, but maybe we could find a way to set aside some time just for us?

HE: (going for a solution) Absolutely. We could make Wednesday our *just us* night. . . .

HOW WE LISTEN

Men and women also have different ways of *showing that they are listening*. Women often respond with verbalizations when listening, such as "um," or "uh-huh." These responses communicate to the other: "I'm listening, go on, I hear you." However, when men use these responses in conversation, they are generally focusing on the content and agreeing with what is being said.

Say a husband is suggesting possible ideas for a vacation site. As he talks, his wife says, "Uh-huh . . . okay . . . yes." He may think she is indicating approval when she is just listening (another example of "what you see is what you get"; he assumes that "yes" means agreement.)

A week later, he comes home with airline tickets to Cancun. She is stunned. "Shouldn't we have discussed this first?"

"But we did," he protests. "I mentioned Cancun, and you said it was okay."

The same couple might have the reverse problem. She comes home from work and starts telling about her day. He listens but does not find any information to say "uh-huh" to. "You're not listening!" she might complain. The fact is, he *was* listening, but he didn't give the signals to show it because he didn't necessarily agree.

Subtle signals are important assurances of safety. A simple "uh-huh" can mean, "I'm with you, you're okay, go on." A wife can feel unsafe when she doesn't get those signals, and a husband can feel double-crossed when the signals are misunderstood.

Approach to a solution: Talk about this issue. Discuss your ways of listening and the kind of cues you want from your spouse.

DETAILS/HIGHLIGHTS

There's another communication difference that often falls along gender lines (though not always). Women tend to remember *details of conversations* while men tend to recall only *what's important to them*. It's feelings and facts again. Women usually gather the whole conversation, including data about the tones and looks and emotional presentation of the speakers. Men usually gather only the information they can use.

They filter out the information they are not interested in.

The classic example is when a friend calls with news of a recent birth.

> HE: Oh, your brother called and said Sally had the baby! A girl. They named her Rebecca!
> SHE: That's wonderful. How much did she weigh?
> HE: Who? Sally?
> SHE: No, silly, *the baby!*
> HE: Oh . . . I don't know.
> SHE: Well, what color hair did she have . . . *the baby!*
> HE: I don't know. Maybe you should call them back.

He thought he had done well to get the sex and the name right. She obviously expected more details.

Have you ever had a conversation like this?

> SHE: What did Fred Morgan have to say?
> HE: He said he was doing okay. He had a few job interviews but nothing good.
> SHE: Where were the interviews?
> HE: I don't know. There was nothing promising.
> SHE: How are he and Julie doing?
> HE: I don't know.
> SHE: So what else did he have to say?
> HE: Not much.
> SHE: You were talking for fifteen minutes. You had to talk about something!

Wives often suspect that their husbands are hiding information by pretending not to remember the details. Especially if there are other safety-threatening factors in the marriage, this brief approach to communication can really bother a wife. She knows that she would gather a pack of details from a fifteen-minute conversation, so she assumes there's something her husband is not telling her.

On the other hand, husbands sometimes suspect their wives of making up details.

Maybe you have had conversations like this:

HE: That's a nice dress.

SHE: You think so? I wasn't sure you'd like it. It's got a lot of red in it.

HE: What's wrong with red?

SHE: You don't like it when I wear red.

HE: When did I say that?

SHE: A couple years ago. We were getting ready for a party and you told me to change out of my red dress because I didn't look good in it.

HE: No, I wouldn't do that.

SHE: You did! You were sitting right there watching TV and you looked over and said red was not my best color.

HE: I did?

SHE: I can't believe you don't remember that. I haven't worn red since.

Memories are funny things. Our recall is based on what we originally perceived and how important it was to us. In a case like this, the wife obviously replayed the scene in her mind whenever she got dressed or went shopping — "mustn't wear red." But the conversation was trivial to the husband, and he quickly forgot it. It's easy to see how conflict might develop out of these differences in memory.

Besides the petty disagreements over who said what when, clashes can erode a couple's trust in each other. A husband may believe his wife would never tell a lie, but he really can't remember the conversation they supposedly had. He wonders if she imagined it or is twisting it to her advantage. Something is terribly wrong, they both assume, when you can't agree on a simple conversation you were both involved in!

But no, it's not any marital skulduggery. They just remember things differently. That's how men and women are made.

Approach to a solution: Give each other the benefit of the doubt. Your spouse is not lying, just remembering differently. When it's important to agree on a past conversation or event, talk through your different versions, including not just facts but also feelings. Try to assemble a fairly reliable account of what took place, and then proceed from there. If it's not important to agree on the old script, just agree to disagree and drop the subject.

PROCESS/PRESENTATION

There's another gender difference that seems more vague, but it affects how men and women interact. It has to do with how we solve problems.

Give a woman a problem to solve and she will, most likely, gather her friends or family to help her. She welcomes other people, including her husband, into the process of problem solving. Together they will find a way.

Give a man a problem to solve and he will, most likely, retreat. *By himself,* he will puzzle it through. Even if he needs help and gets it, he will take that advice and return to his retreat (his cave) and process the problem alone. Once he has the solution, he will return to his family and present it to them, proud of his problem-solving skills.

Consider how this tendency relates to safety issues. How does the woman feel when the man is in his cave solving problems? Anxious. A zillion questions float through her mind. How is he? Will he be able to solve the problem? Will his ideas work? Will he save us? In addition, there

A woman's sense of safety might be threatened by the way her husband solves problems in his life.

may be frustration over being shut out of the process. Even if he has sought her input, he is now rejecting her by figuring things out on his own.

In short, her sense of safety is threatened by the way he solves problems.

How does a man feel when a woman keeps him from going to his cave, when she insists on sharing in the problem-solving process? Now he feels unsafe. What if he proposes a solution that fails? What if she doesn't accept what he says? In the cave, he has the luxury of testing and refining an idea before he presents it, but in the open light of marital conversation, he might put a dumb idea out there for all to see. That makes him nervous.

This pattern of problem solving applies to other areas of life as well—emotions, for instance. Women are (physiologically and culturally) better in touch with their emotions, so they can present their emotions openly, in front of friends and family, and sometimes even strangers. But men need to process their emotions, and they are more comfortable doing this by themselves.

SHE: How do you feel about this?
HE: I don't know how I feel.
SHE: Come on, you can tell me.
HE: I really don't know.

He's right. He doesn't know how he feels. He needs to go to his cave and sort through his emotions. Because she doesn't understand his need, she thinks he is hiding his true feelings. She thinks he has put up a wall to keep her out.

The only wall is his insecurity in dealing with his emotions. He's not as good at expressing his emotions as his wife is. With an overarching need to present himself in a competent way, he's afraid to present his emotions openly before he knows what they are. He might make a fool of himself.

The same pattern often applies to spiritual issues. Women tend to be more open about their spiritual growth. Men need to process it more. In a church small group, a woman is more likely to say, "I'm really struggling with the issue of forgiveness." A man is more likely to say, "I learned something about forgiveness this week." He will not present an idea to others until he has tested it out himself.

In many situations, we find that the very circumstances that threaten him make her feel safe, and vice versa.

SPLITTING THE DIFFERENCES

While these gender differences may create communication difficulties, they are not insurmountable. As stated earlier, if we are to interact with an alien culture, we need to study its customs and language. We have presented some of the basic differences between males and females, but this is just a primer. We need to practice understanding and using the other gender's language—especially during the times when accurate communication is essential to the health and growth of our marriages.

COMMUNICATION DIFFERENCES

FEMALE	MALE
1. Cooperative	Competitive
2. Inclusive	Exclusive
3. Feelings oriented	Facts oriented
4. Relational insights (intuition)	What you see is what you get (information)
5. Listens for details	Listens for what's important to him
6. Processes thoughts and feelings immediately	Needs time to process thoughts and feelings

---

SOLUTION WORKSHOP FIVE

GOAL: Identify gender-based challenges.

In any discussion of gender differences, there are many exceptions. Do not assume that everything we have written is true of you or your spouse. Look over the following list and check those that apply to your relationship:

☐ She: Cooperative   ☐ He: Competitive

☐ She: Inclusive   ☐ He: Exclusive

☐ She: Feelings   ☐ He: Facts

☐ She: Relational insights (intuition)   ☐ He: What you see is what you get (information)

☐ She: Listens for details   ☐ He: Listens for what's important to him

☐ She: Processes thoughts and feelings immediately   ☐ He: Needs time to process his thoughts and feelings

1. How would you describe your ability to express emotions?

   For the Wife
   - ☐ I express emotions fully and frequently.
   - ☐ I express emotions easily, but try to hold back for my husband's sake.
   - ☐ I express some emotions pretty easily.
   - ☐ I find some emotions difficult to express.
   - ☐ I get embarrassed when I express my emotions.
   - ☐ I express my emotions sometimes, but in a very careful, guarded way.
   - ☐ I find it difficult to express my emotions.
   - ☐ I'm just not very emotional.
   - ☐ Other (name it):

   For the Husband
   - ☐ I express emotions fully and frequently.
   - ☐ I express emotions easily, but I try to hold back for my wife's sake.
   - ☐ I express some emotions pretty easily.
   - ☐ I find some emotions difficult to express.
   - ☐ I get embarrassed when I express my emotions.
   - ☐ I express my emotions sometimes, but in a very careful, guarded way.
   - ☐ I find it difficult to express my emotions.
   - ☐ I'm just not very emotional.
   - ☐ Other (name it):

2. Of all the gender differences we have discussed, in what areas does your marriage *not* fit the mold?

3. Has there been an incident in your marriage in the last month that you could attribute to one of the gender differences described in this chapter? What happened?

4. Knowing what you know now, would you do anything differently? If so, what?

For the Wife

5. Of the tendencies we have discussed in this chapter, is there one that you'd like to change in yourself? Which one?

6. What difference would this change make in your behavior or conversation?

7. Is there one tendency that you'd like your husband to change, even slightly? Which one?

8. What difference would this change make in your husband's behavior or conversation?

For the Husband

5. Of the tendencies we have discussed in this chapter, is there one that you'd like to change in yourself? Which one?

6. What difference would this change make in your behavior or conversation?

7. Is there one tendency that you'd like your wife to change, even slightly? Which one?

8. What difference would this change make in your wife's behavior or conversation?

For Both

9. Write a short script of a *typical* conversation in your home — *without adding the four changes you just described.* Then rewrite the script *with the changes* and show how those changes affect the conversation.

▼ ▼

Creative Communication

The funny thing about communication is that, whether we know it or not, we are always communicating. It is impossible *not* to communicate.

Communication involves what you say, how you look, and what you do. Silence can speak as loudly as the most vehement tirade. A simple look can say more than a sermon. One only needs to speak to a parent of a teenage child to realize how much can be spoken by the smallest gestures—rolling of the eyes, a curl of the lip, or an unfettered smile.

In marriage, a husband and wife are always communicating. When everything is going well, maybe during the romantic stage, this doesn't present much of a problem. Both parties are so certain that the other will meet their needs (and are so anesthetized to the negatives) that their communication is generally positive. However, think about the impact of continual communication when the marriage reaches the stage of conflict or negotiation. The irritable look, the silence, the lack of touch—all of these communicate. Often we are not even aware that communication is occurring.

But let's take it to the next step. Say Larry sends a sneer to his wife Linda without even knowing it. Linda then reacts to his communication with a cold shoulder, leaving Larry wondering, "What's her problem?"

One well-known biblical phrase is "speaking the truth in love" (Ephesians 4:15). In a just a few words, the phrase says volumes about how to conduct relationships. Paul was writing to the Ephesians about relationships within the church, but we can borrow the phrase as an ideal for marriage. We want to make sure the proper message is coming through (truth), but

In marriage, a husband and wife are always communicating. Often they are unaware of what they are conveying.

we also want to make sure it is delivered in a loving manner. Message and manner are both crucial concerns as we seek to speak the truth in love.

This concept was made clear to me in one counseling session with a couple I* was working with on the issue of communication. Dave worked a job that required him to commute about an hour a day each way on primarily two-lane roads. His wife, Anne, worked part time as an accountant about ten minutes from home. Dave worked a labor-intensive job as a plant manager and found the commute a very difficult way to end his day. As a result, he would often arrive home frustrated and distressed.

He developed a routine in which he would walk through the door, pick up the mail, and head up to his study. None of his actions were directly related to how he felt about Anne. But, she hadn't seen him all day, looked forward to talking to him, and was hurt and angered by his behavior.

Why? To her, his silence and avoidance upon arriving home communicated that she was unimportant. Of course, she reacted angrily. In therapy, Dave came to understand that, even though he was not planning to communicate anything when he came home and went to his room, he was still communicating. Once he realized this, he could make sure he communicated the love and care he felt.

---

*All first person pronouns in this chapter refer to Tom Bartlett.

FALSE ASSUMPTIONS

Deborah Tannen is a linguist who has written a couple of best sellers on the subject of conversation style and relationships.[1] She states that people tend to communicate based on two major false assumptions about communication:

1. *I assume that what I communicate to you will be understood by you in the same manner as I understand it.* In other words, when Anne told Dave that it bothered her when he came home from work and went right upstairs, she assumed that he would understand that she was hurt, sad, and felt unloved. Dave, however, understood Anne to be angry, telling him that he never did anything right.

2. *I also assume that I can ask you what you want and you will tell me.* To understand this assumption, just think about how many times your spouse has asked you what was wrong or what you wanted. If you're like most people, you usually reply, "Oh, nothing." If you are going to begin to communicate in a healthy manner with your spouse, you need to recognize that communication takes work. We do not automatically have a shared understanding of communication. And even when asked, we are often indirect in responding.

People assume that if they can communicate safely and speak honestly, they will be understood charitably. But this is not always the case. As you may know, when a marriage is strained even the simplest conversation can be a battle.

INTENTIONS AND CHARACTER

How do we establish safety in our communication? We must deal with *intentions* and *character.*

Intention is what a person means to do or say. Character refers to someone's life traits—for instance, selfishness or greed or innocence. We regularly view the actions of others and ourselves according to these two factors—intentions and character. Unfortunately, most of us have a double standard, which can sabotage communication.

Research indicates that we are strongly biased toward ourselves. We generally take our good character and good intentions for granted. *I'm really a nice person,* you might think. *When I said that about Bob, it might have come out wrong. But I didn't mean to hurt his feelings.* When we do something wrong or hurtful, we tend to blame it on circumstances rather than accusing ourselves of being mean or selfish. Since we know our own intentions, we excuse ourselves rather easily.

However, when others hurt *our* feelings, it's a different story. We doubt their good intentions and reject possible excuses. Instead, we assume that they have character flaws.

Many misunderstandings occur because one person is reaching wrong conclusions about another. If someone bumps you as you walk on the sidewalk, you might consider the person rude or mean—you might even shove the person back. But if *you* are carrying a heavy shopping bag and accidentally jostle someone else on that same sidewalk, well, it was an accident. The person you bumped may give you a dirty look, so you respond, "Hey, give me a break! I'm trying to carry something here! I didn't mean it!"

Your motives and intentions, which are so obvious to you, are not always perceived by those around you. This is true on city sidewalks and in marriages. Misunderstandings will arise in your marriage. They are inevitable. Your spouse will make a comment, and you will hear something else. It doesn't mean that either of you are crazy, crafty, or cruel—it just happens. You will be hurt by things that your spouse says in innocence, and you will unwittingly hurt your spouse.

How can you deal with these misunderstandings? In our solution approach, the answer is fairly simple: You start by giving each other the benefit of the doubt.

Remember the safety contract? In it, you both declared your intentions not to hurt each other. Trust in the commitment. It's the old *act-as-if technique* often used in solution-based therapy. Even if you harbor suspicions about your spouse's motives, act as if you believe your spouse meant well.

You need to get to a point where you recognize that you both generally have good intentions. You are not *trying* to hurt each other. If you can affirm each other's basic character, you can avoid the snap reactions that escalate conflict. If you allow one another the same excuses you allow yourselves, you can keep the peace long enough to hear what was really meant.

THE LIMITS OF LANGUAGE

Have you ever had a feeling that you didn't know how to describe? You just don't have the words for it. The feeling—pain or love or anger or hope—was very real to you, but describing it went beyond language.

Our body language will often speak louder than our words.

Have you ever said one thing and meant another? Whether you were just being polite or just plain lying, you said something you thought you *should* say, even though it wasn't the way you honestly felt. Sometimes you may even try to talk *yourself* into something that you may not really feel—like the weight-watcher who lunches on celery and tofu and says, "Mmm, tasty," even though that feeling doesn't exist.

Language is limited. The majority of what we communicate is not in the dictionary definition of the words we say, but in the way we say them and in the things we do. Tone of voice, facial expression, inflection, and body posture all can send a stronger message than the words we say.

A wife approaches her husband about a problem and he becomes defensive. "Why are you getting so angry?" she asks.

"I am not angry!" the husband growls through clenched teeth with a tight jaw and a red face.

Which speaks louder? The words "I am not angry" or the gestures, tone, and behavior accompanying the message? Often, it's the behavior and signals that accompany the message that provide the real meaning. It's called a nonverbal communication—between the lines, under the surface, beyond words.

INTIMACY AND AUTONOMY

Here's the problem: We are all sending nonverbal messages without knowing it. We can plan what words we say, but we can't always control the nuances of voice and behavior that relay it. Those signals are a kind of lie detector—perhaps we should say a truth detector—because they often give a fuller picture of the true feelings behind our words.

Let's consider two types of people in this world. Some want *intimacy* while others want *autonomy*. Most people have both desires in different proportions. But here's one of those gender generalizations: Women tend to be more on the intimacy-craving side while men tend to want autonomy more.

If you thrive on intimacy, how do you feel about nonverbal communication? You love it. Nonverbal signals are the windows into the soul. They are how you really know your spouse. He may guard his words carefully, but he speaks volumes with his actions, expressions, posture, and tone of voice.

If you favor autonomy, how do you feel about nonverbal communication? You are threatened by it, because you cannot control it. You want to focus on the words you choose to say, not on the subtle nuances of how your lip curled when you said them.

Therefore, these two people communicate on different levels. Mr. Autonomy (yes, I'm using those gender stereotypes) goes for the bottom line—"Just the facts, Ma'am." Mrs. Intimacy functions on the level of looks and tone. This is why the same words can mean entirely different things to them—and to you and your spouse.

SCENE A
SHE: So, do you want to go to the Smiths' party?
HE: Sure, let's go.
SHE: You don't want to go, do you?
HE: Sure I do. It'll be fun.
SHE: I know you don't like the Smiths very much, but she's my boss, and we really ought to be there.
HE: Fine.
SHE: It won't be that bad.

She is picking up cues and clues beyond the words that are spoken. He is operating on a more literal level. Reading the words on paper, we might think that the woman in the scene is not really listening, but we're not getting the full force of the conversation—the tone of voice, the look in his eyes, and so forth. She is actually listening very well, but under the surface of the language itself.

When he says he wants to go to the party, she reads the opposite message. He may be perturbed by this. Maybe he really doesn't want to go, but he has decided to be a good husband and go along willingly. He has chosen (autonomously) to say "yes" to this party. But she reads his nonverbal communication and understands his reluctance. That can be a bit unnerving.

SCENE B
SHE: How do I look?
HE: Fine.
SHE: Fine?
HE: Yeah, you look nice.
SHE: Nice?
HE: Uh huh, that's a nice outfit.
SHE: I'd better change.

When "he" says her outfit is fine and nice, she hears that it is "only adequate." She wants to wear something smashing, not run-of-the-mill. He intends a compliment, but clothes aren't that important to him, so he doesn't know the right vocabulary. She is looking for affirmation from him, and she doesn't get it. In fact, she may even be upset at him for this, and he has no idea why.

SCENE C
SHE: Did you see the Morgans in church today?
HE: Yep. I talked with Fred for a while.
SHE: He still doesn't have a job, does he?
HE: No, he doesn't. But he's doing okay. He got a pretty good severance package.
SHE: I'm worried about them. He seems depressed.
HE: Don't worry. He's doing fine. He told me so himself.

He talked with Fred Morgan, and Fred said everything was fine. On a purely literal level of conversation, he accepts that. No need to worry; Fred's okay. But she saw Fred across the church lobby and immediately saw a pack of indicators that all was *not* well. Fred looked depressed, and she worries about him. The husband, autonomous as always, wonders why they can't just let Fred decide how he is, while the wife realizes that men will often hide their true needs.

Misunderstandings like these are not signs that your marriage is disintegrating. Nor are they signs that your spouse just doesn't want to communicate. They are natural and normal.

DANCES WITH EXPECTATIONS

Most communication is actually an intricate dance of *responding to expectations.*

Jim and Sally demonstrated this dance very well. Both expressed hurt and anger about Jim's late arrival home after work. Inevitably, he would receive a phone call or unexpected visitor near the end of his workday, making him leave work late and arrive home later than expected. Sally, in the meantime, would eagerly anticipate his arrival, wanting to be with him, to have him spend some time with the children, and to eat their evening meal together. Over the course of this marriage, Sally was disappointed again and again when Jim was late.

Expectations. Jim expected some understanding—it wasn't his fault that a client called at 4:55—but he received only blame. Sally expected to be important to Jim—important enough for him to come home on time—but she received only more disappointment.

The ironic thing about these expectations was that both Jim and Sally were experiencing hurt or anger because they looked forward to being with the other. The underlying motivation was to show love for their mate. However, whenever Jim was delayed, he knew what to expect from Sally. As he drove home, he would begin a mental argument with her, telling her how hard he worked and that he didn't enjoy taking late phone calls—and by the time he walked through the door he had ammunition ready.

At the same time, Sally went through a similar exercise. She would go over in her mind how hard she had worked, and how he didn't understand how much she looked forward to seeing him, and how frustrating the kids had been, and how much she wanted to have an adult conversation. She anticipated how he would be abrupt, how he would not listen. As she thought about this, she became more frustrated and discouraged. Inevitably, they were like two trains on the same track headed toward a collision—all set up by their expectations.

Most communication is actually an intricate dance of responding to expectations.

Clearly, Jim and Sally have two sets of expectations. First there are the good expectations: the care and understanding that these two partners should expect from each other. But their expectations were dashed, causing pain and disappointment. As a result there are negative expectations. Both expect to be hurt. Both expect a fight. The result is that they fulfill the other's negative expectations, even though neither intends to hurt the other.

The dance began to change when each was willing to take responsibility for his or her own behavior, when they began to recognize that they had the power and ability to communicate differently, and when they began to give each other the benefit of the doubt. They learned to recognize that they did not always correctly interpret their partner's intentions. They learned to peer through those all-too-common misunderstandings.

ACTIVE LISTENING

The book of Proverbs says, "He who answers before listening— that is his folly and his shame" (18:13). Often when we think of communication we focus on how things are said—the skill in saying things—but the true key of communication is *listening*. If we want to find solutions to our communication problems, we must learn to listen.

Most of us do not think of listening as a skill. We automatically do it because we are human. However, you could probably think of an incident or two within the last week where you did not listen fully to some communication, which resulted in misunderstanding or confusion. We need to train our "listening muscles." Like our physical bodies, if we do not practice listening, the muscles atrophy and become ineffective.

Think for a moment about how most of us listen. If someone is speaking, we usually begin to formulate a response before the person is finished. Sometimes we even interrupt him with our responses, as soon as we gather the gist of what he is saying.

A common complaint of couples who come for marital therapy is "My spouse does not listen!" Why is this such a deep-felt need? It goes back to our basic needs to love, be loved, and feel worthwhile and competent. Listening is a skill that most closely addresses these needs. When you truly listen to your spouse—in a way that you hear what he or she says and feels without judgment and criticism—you are helping your spouse feel loved and worthwhile.

One technique we often use with couples is the sounding board described at the end of this chapter. It is a repetition exercise—no questions, no criticisms—one partner merely repeats what the other has said. Often, after this exercise, a husband will say that he found out things about how his wife feels that he never knew before, or a wife will say that she never felt as nurtured and cared for as when her spouse listened to her.

"He who answers before listening—that is his folly and his shame" (Proverbs 18:13).

Of course, in order to learn this skill one needs to know the components. The kind of listening is *active listening*. Active listening involves paying attention to the nonverbal signals as well as the message.

All of us have tried to do two things at the same time—"listening" while doing something else. A husband may sit at the breakfast table glancing at the paper while his wife is talking over their morning coffee. When she says, "You're not listening to me," he immediately responds defensively and somewhat smugly, "Oh, yes, I am," and then parrots back perfectly the last sentence or two that she said. The fact is, we have amazing minds that have the ability to pick up information around us and hold it briefly in our memory. *This is not the same as listening.* Although this husband knows the words his wife said, that's all he knows. He was not focused on his wife, reading her nonverbal signals, nodding, or responding. The focus of his mental energy was on a different subject—and this was obvious to her by the nonverbal communication she read on his face.

Active listening is a crucial skill for the preservation and growth of any marriage. In trying to explain and teach this skill, I have found it helpful to divide active listening into two parts: the *context* (surrounding events) and the *content* (message).

THE CONTEXT

In order to have healthy, creative communication, you need to become a keen observer of the *context* of your conversations. You must learn to read your spouse's body language, facial expression, voice tone, and inflection.

> SHE: We need to talk.
> HE: (without taking his eyes off the ball game on TV)
> All right. Let's talk.

Later, when this wife complains that he never wants to communicate with her, the husband may innocently say, "What's the problem? I said we could talk." He said it, but he didn't *show* it. This husband is apparently ignorant of his own nonverbal communication (unless of course he intended to put forth that mixed signal).

CONTEXT-BASED SOLUTIONS FOR IMPROVING COMMUNICATION

Couples who are unaware of the context of their messages will experience regular misunderstandings, frustrations, and difficulties in communication. Too often couples get trapped in cycles of miscommunication. They focus only on their disappointment and anger—"We just don't click! We're talking right past each other!" It can be frightening when something as

seemingly simple as communication isn't working anymore.

But in our solution approach, we go back to basics. There is hope for your communication. You *can* learn to understand each other, but you need to break your old patterns and develop new ones. Of course you won't be expert at the new patterns right away, but as you practice, you'll get the hang of them.

1. Pay attention to your underlying messages. Begin to take a look at how you communicate. Learn to observe the context as well as the content in your conversations. As previously said, we often don't realize all the nonverbal signals we're sending—even though these may seriously hurt our marital communication.

Think back over some recent misunderstandings you have had. How did your message match up with your nonverbal communication? Were your body language, look, and tone of voice all agreeing with your words?

Please notice that this is *self*-observation. Don't start picking at your partner. Focus on yourself, what *you* did or said, what *you* need to change. As you monitor your own behavior, you can learn more about the context of what you're saying. That will give you great insight into what your spouse is hearing.

But you need to go beyond mere monitoring. Make it a point to listen and talk to your spouse with your whole body. Don't hide behind your reading material or focus on the television. Look your partner in the eye, turn your body in his or her direction, and lean forward. This will seem odd to begin with, but as you develop the pattern, it will become a natural aid to your conversation.

2. Learn to read your spouse's underlying messages. Maybe you already do this very well, but maybe not. If you're the bottom-line type, who hears only the content and not the context, you need to start paying attention to those physical, facial, and vocal clues that let you know what's really going on.

Often one spouse will test the other by saying that everything's fine, while sending an underlying message of "Help!" But what he or she says is, "Don't mind me. I'll just sit over here by myself, all alone, while you watch your TV show. I'm sure I can think of something to do. Don't worry, I'll be fine. Wouldn't want you to miss that important program."

You get the idea. The words say one thing, but everything about the presentation of those words says another. The point is: If you really cared enough to pay attention to me, you would pick up my nonverbal signals and see that something's wrong.

Get beyond the words-only understanding. Study your spouse as you would a good mystery novel, and learn to pick up all the clues.

3. Bring the underlying messages to the surface. To improve your marital communication, you need to talk about what you both *mean*. You need to bring those unconscious, unspoken messages to a conscious, spoken level. Begin to identify when your words do not match your body language. If your spouse is sending mixed messages, talk about it openly.

This might be difficult, especially if you have a well-ingrained habit of stuffing your true feelings below the surface. It may seem strange to you to say: "I want to talk to you about something that's bothering me, but I'm not sure I know how to say it right. I don't mean to hurt you, but if I say something that bothers you, let me know and we'll talk about it." Or, "When I see the way you're sitting there, it makes me think something's not right here."

We have found that *open-ended statements* work much better than *direct questions* with most couples. To ask, "How are you really feeling?" may elicit a defensive or evasive response. But when you say what you see, you can show interest in the other person without giving a sense of criticism or interrogation.

For example, if your spouse comes home from work visibly irritated, rather than asking him or her what's wrong or if it was a bad day at work, try something like this: "Hi, honey, it looks as if you've had a tough day." This has a number of effects.

1. It allows your spouse to know that you have some sense of how he or she is feeling.
2. It keeps you from being just one more person in this busy day bugging him or her with questions.
3. It presents an accepting, noncritical spirit.
4. You give permission for your spouse to respond or not to respond.

The open-ended statement is clearly an *observation* rather than an *accusation*. It is an "I message." The speaker is taking responsibility for his or her own interpretation of and response to a message given previously by another person, without imputing negative intentions to the other person. If a wife rushes in after work and immediately checks her phone messages before kissing her husband, the husband might say, "I feel neglected when you do that. I feel as if your messages are more important than I am." Notice that the husband is not assuming anything about his wife's intentions, just expressing how he feels.

An *I message* allows you to describe your observation, the message you're getting, and the feelings you have about it without placing blame. It does not make the other person the bad guy, but it does identify the problem. The problem might be a behavior that needs modification or an interpretation of the behavior that needs to be clarified.

Time and time again we have seen spouses, even some who had been withholding communication, respond very favorably when they received the acceptance and freedom to respond that an open-ended statement provides.

4. Determine to make some changes. You can be a thermometer or a thermostat. A thermometer simply reacts to the temperature; a thermostat changes it. How can you and your spouse stop merely reacting to each other's communication styles and start really communicating? Decide together what changes you both need to make.

As you become more aware of the context of your conversations with your spouse, when speaking or listening, you can work to make your nonverbal signals confirm, rather than contradict, your spoken messages. This may take some practice, but it will improve your communication immensely.

Jerry's wife complained that he never seemed to spend time with her or their children. He would come home from the office, eat, and then return phone calls from work in the evening. He protested that he *did* spend time with Jane, but she said he always seemed distracted, as if he had better things to do. After discussing the issue of nonverbal communication and context, we suggested some possible changes in his behavior that would send different messages to Jane.

At their next session, Jane stated that the changes were working. She said Jerry had spent a lot more time with her and it had been a good, positive time for them. Jerry was pleased to hear this, but still, he was surprised that she said he was spending a lot more time with her. He was a bottom-line kind of guy. He knew how many hours and minutes they had been together. Their actual time together had not increased all that much.

Jerry slowly recognized that every minute gained value when he changed his tone, his eye contact, and his body language to show his wife that he cared about what she was saying. From an accounting standpoint he may not have spent any more time with her, but she felt the time truly *with* her had increased greatly.

5. Avoid "megadosing." One of the most common responses we humans make is to "megadose" the problem. Most of us are smart enough not to megadose medication—"If one aspirin didn't get rid of my headache, then maybe twenty will." However, when it comes to human relationships, we don't seem to figure this out very well.

Earlier in this chapter we met Dave and Anne. Anne would repeatedly tell Dave how disappointed she was that he came home and went right to his room, not talking to her, not asking about her day. In response he would get angry, retreat even more, sharing even less with her. The more she talked at him, the less he talked. She was megadosing and things were only getting worse. He began to make changes in the direction she wanted only when she stopped nagging him and began to approach him positively.

This leads us to another significant way of changing the dance of failed communication—focusing on small changes. Dave and Anne were able to make small changes in the dance they played out each day. In our session, Dave agreed to try a new approach. When he came home from work, instead of expecting the worst from Anne and greeting her accordingly, he decided to greet her with a hug and a kiss. He also agreed to take a few minutes to ask about her day before he went to change his clothes. His willingness to make this small change brought an equal change and reaction from Anne. She started to feel more important to Dave and was less critical. He began to look forward to coming home, which led to additional reciprocal changes.

UNDERSTANDING THE CONTEXT

1. Pay attention to your underlying messages.
2. Learn to read your spouse's underlying messages.
3. Bring the underlying messages to the surface.
4. Determine to make some changes.
5. Avoid *megadosing*.

THE CONTENT

After recognizing that an open-ended statement provides the door through which you can walk into healthy communication, you have to deal with the *content* of what you and your spouse are saying.

Probably the most significant tool for developing good listening skills is *reflection*. When you look into a mirror, you see a reflection closely resembling your own image. In conversation, you can practice effective listening by restating to the other person your understanding of what you just heard.

As marital therapists, we have found a number of reasons why reflection works so well. Reflection lets other people know that you have actually heard what they have said. If you are able to restate their message accurately, then you must have been listening.

Second, restatement allows the speaker to feel heard without being criticized. Too often, we jump to judgment of what others say, even before they're finished speaking. (On daytime TV talk shows, you can watch all day without hearing anyone complete a sentence.) In the process, people are often misunderstood. But if you restate what you hear, it forces you as the listener to slow your mental processes and take the time to focus thoroughly on what the speaker is saying.

But reflection is not only parroting back the *words* that the person has said, but also restating the *emotional context* of the message. This can be very helpful in getting messages across clearly.

We might think of two people talking as if they were two fax machines. Fax A has an image—a picture, or a typed page—that contains information that needs to get to fax B. The document is placed into the fax machine, and the image is decoded by the fax machine and transformed into small pieces of electrical information that are sent across telephone wires to fax B. Fax B takes those bits of electrical information, reassembles them into the same image, and produces a piece of paper that (we hope) looks similar to the one that was originally entered into fax A.

Unfortunately, fax machines don't always work perfectly. Occasionally you may get a call or return fax from the person receiving your transmission: "There is some distortion—could you send it through again?"

How are human beings like fax machines?

We too have images and information in our minds that we have to transform into bits for transmission—only we are vocally producing sound waves rather than electronic signals. The bits are sent through the air to a person who receives the sound waves, takes the bits of information, and tries to reassemble the original idea. As with the fax transmission, sometimes the message is a bit distorted or garbled.

As we learned early in this chapter, we tend to assume that other people perceive words and meanings just as we perceive them—just as people tend to assume that faxes always get sent perfectly. However, this is not always the case. That's why restating the content and context of the message helps person A to know if there has been some distortion in the transmission to person B. If there's a problem, person A can retransmit—express the idea again—until it is accurately received by person B.

THE ANGER FACTOR

Anger often prevents communication, but not always in the way you might think. The *fear of anger* keeps many couples from fully expressing their feelings. We may be afraid that, if we begin to talk about our pent-up frustrations and disappointments, we will lose control. We don't want anger to engulf us. We're afraid we'll do or say something that will destroy the marriage.

As a result, marriages often rot from within, as fear of anger blocks any true communication. The walls set up to contain the anger actually serve to separate the two partners. We *can* break down the walls if we learn more about what anger is and how we can deal with it.

Anger is usually a secondary emotion, often a shield against other emotions that we do not know how to express or that are too hurtful to express. When I was a child, I shared a bedroom with my older brother. On one occasion, as I entered the room to go to bed, my older brother (God bless him!) jumped from behind the door, yelling, "Boo!" as loudly as he could. The first *conscious thought* I had was an intense urge to wring his scrawny neck. I was angry. I was ready to fight.

However, my anger was not the first *emotion* that I felt. My first emotion was fear. I was scared out of my wits. Fear energized my anger. It was too embarrassing to let my brother know that he had "gotten" me, so my recourse was to become angry and try to fight him.

As couples, we need to learn that *appropriately expressed* anger is important and acceptable in developing healthy communication. Anger itself is usually just the tip of the iceberg. We see our craggy anger looming before us, but below the water line is hurt, fear, sadness, tiredness, and other similar emotions. If we never allow each other (or ourselves) to express appropriate anger, we cannot identify those other emotions that need to be resolved in our relationships.

What does this have to do with active listening and reflection? Well, some people do pretty well with these methods — until they see that anger-iceberg approaching. Then they panic, resorting to old habits. But recognizing, expressing, and resolving anger can all be part of the active listening process.

When Jim is late again, he can say to Sally, "It sounds to me as if you're angry with me for coming home late." That gives Sally the opportunity to state that, yes, she is angry, but that she is also frightened regarding Jim's well-being (or hurt that he didn't consider her feelings enough to call and say he'd be late).

Through reflection, they can get to the real issue, which allows them to make the behavior changes that will heal their relationship. In fact, this was the kind of approach that got Jim and Sally back on track.

The fear of anger keeps many couples from fully expressing their feelings.

The end of this chapter provides some exercises to improve your communication skills. As you work to communicate effectively you may notice improvement, but you will find that areas of conflict and relationship difficulty continue to exist. In the next section, you will look at the patterns of conflict that many couples experience as well as learning the tools to change these patterns and effectively resolve conflicts.

HELPFUL HINTS FOR EFFECTIVE COMMUNICATION

1. Timing: Timing is, as they say, everything. And there are times when one partner or the other is too tired, too distracted, or too angry to do the work of real communication. Learn to recognize those times. It's all right to reschedule a much-needed talk for a better time—just make sure you don't put it off indefinitely. It's okay to say, "There is something I would like to talk to you about but I know that now is not a good time. Could we discuss it tomorrow at dinner?"

2. Four magic words: John Gray describes four magic words that men and women can use to help defuse some of the gender differences that can cause conflict in communication. Men, he says, tend to think they are being blamed when a woman shares her feelings and thoughts about a problem. (They hear: "I'm unhappy about this. What are you going to do about it?") Wives, it can be very helpful to add four magic words when sharing your feelings with your husband: *It's* *not your fault.* It will help him realize that he does not need to be defensive or to try to fix the problem. It gives him the freedom to listen. Try telling him that he is actually helping you by listening to you.[2]

3. *Four more magic words:* According to Gray, men frequently withdraw and spend time in their caves by themselves. It's alone time that men seem to need at a visceral level (though some more than others). Women, generally more social creatures, don't always understand this. In fact, many women become anxious when men withdraw or seek their own space—they worry that men are drifting away from them. So Gray suggests that men employ four magic words of their own: *I will be back.* If you learn to recognize when you need to go off on your own, you can ease the way by offering this reassurance, indicating that you are willing to communicate, just not now.[3]

4. *Positive reinforcement:* Researchers at the University of Washington were able to predict with 94 percent accuracy those couples in their study who would later divorce. The one determining factor that led to their accuracy was the ratio of positive statements to negative statements that spouses made to each other. They found that the optimal ratio was five positive statements to one negative. In healthy couples, partners gave each other "five compliments for each noncommittal answer or complaint: five expressions of affection for every outburst of anger or blame; five good things for every bad. The lesson? People need warm, positive reinforcement from their partners in order to stay the course."[4] The moral is that, in spite of the techniques noted throughout this chapter, one of the best ways to begin to effect positive change in your marriage is to make the commitment to become a positive spouse—someone who looks for ways to provide praise and reinforcement to the other.

SOLUTION WORKSHOP SIX

GOAL: To improve communication skills.

Exercise One: The B-E-A-R Method

The following acronym—B-E-A-R—may help you remember the skills needed to describe your observations and your feelings in a positive, healthy, manner.

Choose a recent event that caused you to experience some emotion toward your spouse and complete the four components.

B (Behavior) Describe the behavior that occurred (words, actions, etc.). *Example:* This morning you left for work without saying goodbye.

E (Emotion) Describe the feeling you had about the behavior. *Example:* I felt sad and hurt. I felt like you didn't care.

A (Alternative) Describe how you would like it to have been, an alternative behavior you would prefer. *Example:* I would appreciate it if you would say goodbye to me before you leave for work in the morning.

R (Result) Describe the consequence that will result from your spouse acting on your requested alternative. *Example:* If you would do that for me, I would really appreciate it and it would help me feel closer to you.

The B-E-A-R is an excellent tool to help you organize your thoughts and feelings. You can utilize this format to help you develop healthy "I messages" in preparation for talking with your partner. It can also be used as a way of writing a note in an organized manner when communicating in written form is safer or more appropriate.

If your spouse is willing, it can be a very helpful exercise to have each of you pick an event, possibly a conflict that has occurred, and separately complete this exercise. Share what you have written with each other and take time to think about the other person's perspective.[5]

Exercise Two: Listening Exercise (Sounding Board)
Listening is a skill that few of us have been taught and even fewer of us practice. The following exercise is intended to provide a simple way to practice listening. You will need to practice—it may be a simple exercise but it is harder to do than it seems.[6]

1. One of you is the designated speaker and the other has the role of being the listener—the sounding board.
2. The speaker is to talk about something that occurred during the day, starting with a brief statement. (Today at work [this happened] and I was upset about it.)
3. The listener is to send back to the speaker a brief statement summarizing what was heard. (So you are saying that at work today you were upset about. . . .) *Note:* The listener may not ask questions, give suggestions, or critique what the speaker has said. The sounding board can simply paraphrase to the speaker the message and emotion he or she heard from the speaker.
4. The speaker continues to make brief statements of clarification on the same topic, which are reflected back by the listener.
5. The purpose of this exercise is not to resolve conflict or solve problems, but to have the speaker feel fully listened to by the spouse (possibly for the first time in quite some time without criticism or at least with full and undivided attention). The exercise is considered complete when the speaker can say to the listener, "That's right, now you know exactly how I feel."
6. Reverse roles so that each partner has the opportunity to both practice active listening and experience being listened to in a nonjudgmental manner. Give each partner equal time in each role.

After this technique is mastered, you can do this together to gain understanding of more difficult issues.

Exercise Three: Empathy Exercise
This exercise will help each of you come to an understanding of what your spouse is feeling about an issue. It is important to recognize that empathy is not the same as sympathy. Empathy is the ability to put yourself in the other person's place (whether you agree or not), experiencing what they might feel in the situation.

Attempt the following together:

1. Think of a recent concern or conflict that you and your spouse experienced. Write down how you think your spouse sees the issue by answering the following questions.

   - ▾ What does he or she think about the issue?
   - ▾ What does it mean to him or her?
   - ▾ If I were him or her, what would I want?
   - ▾ If I were him or her, how would I feel?
   - ▾ In her or his place, what would my intention be?

2. Answering the same questions, write down how you see the issue.

3. Share your responses with your spouse. Remember that there are no right or wrong answers. Take time to share and talk about those areas where your spouse seemed to understand you and those areas where he or she did not.

PART THREE

Solution-Based Techniques for Resolving Conflicts

▼ ▼

CHAPTER SEVEN

What Doesn't Work: Destructive Patterns in Conflict Resolution

Frank grew up in a home with a lot of conflict. His father was an alcoholic, and Frank learned to cope by withdrawing to his room and shutting out the rest of the world. Today, Frank is not much different. His wife, Nancy, is not an alcoholic, but she is very assertive, regularly confronting him about his manners, his dress, and his personality. Frank deals with this criticism by withdrawing. At first he went into the family room and read the paper or watched a ball game on television. But his withdrawal only made Nancy angrier, so she would follow him.

As you might expect, Frank just learned new ways of finding the peace he was seeking. He shut down emotionally. He purchased a Walkman with earphones and proceeded to walk around the house with his earphones on most of the time. He avoided mealtimes by working extra hours, and he avoided bedtime by staying up late to watch cable movies. All of these were Frank's ways of avoiding any face-to-face confrontation.

Nancy saw that she couldn't make Frank interact with her, so she turned her anger inward and consequently became very depressed. By the time she came for counseling, she was seeking anti-depressants and a divorce.

Chuck and Lois were much different. Chuck also grew up in an angry household, but he seemed to be repeating the pattern, showing anger easily when things weren't going well. Most people consider Chuck a strong leader. He heads up his own company and manages most things he gets involved with, including his family.

Submissive by nature, Lois was attracted to Chuck's aggressive qualities, wishing she were more that way. But of course, after the wedding, she learned that there was a down side to his leadership. Chuck could become very bossy and controlling.

We all have destructive tendencies that creep to the surface from time to time. Left unchecked, they can destroy our relationships.

Lois reacted by not criticizing or challenging him at all. After all, she wanted to be a submissive, godly wife. Over time Chuck saw her submissive response as a weakness. He lost respect for her and began to treat her as a child, belittling her in public and scolding her in private. His lack of respect for his wife evolved into a destructive pattern. Lois lost all confidence in herself, feeling as if she were incapable of even simple tasks such as writing checks or shopping.

Chuck found other women he admired and flaunted these women and all their attributes in front of Lois. When Lois came to see me* she said she wished she were dead.

WHERE BAD PATTERNS COME FROM

Clearly, the previous examples are destructive patterns. Your marriage may not be as bad as the examples above, but we all have destructive tendencies that creep to the surface from time to time. Left unchecked, they can destroy our relationships. Usually these patterns evolve so gradually that we are the last ones to recognize them.

Where do we learn these destructive patterns? From the homes we lived in as we grew up.

There are two unhealthy models of conflict management

---

*All first person pronouns in this chapter refer to Tom Whiteman.

in homes. The first is *avoidance*. Many families tiptoe through their disagreements, careful not to bring up anything that might cause a fight. This style is typical of homes with addictions or other major dysfunctions. You don't talk about the real problem. Kids from these homes grow up with no tools for resolving disagreements, just a deep fear of conflict.

The second model is *explosion*. In these homes, someone is always fighting with someone else. Angry words abound, sometimes accompanied by violent actions. They never really resolve conflict, they just have to talk louder or act stronger than everyone else. Seeing the damage done by unchecked tempers, many kids grow up wanting to avoid conflict at all costs (although some go to the other extreme, continuing the explosive pattern in their own lives).

Neither of these models involves a *healthy* disagreement. One model is engaging in a world war, complete with emotional explosions and sometimes physical violence. The other is stuffing true feelings under a veil of silence, until the feelings seep out in passive-aggressive sabotage or just rot the spirit.

Unfortunately, many homes have fallen into one or another of these destructive patterns. Whether explosive or avoidant, the patterns produce people who *don't do conflict*. They aren't learning ways to get *through* disagreements; they either blast their opponents or try to walk by on the other side.

That means that you, as you seek solutions to your marital conflicts, may be writing a new script. Chances are, your parents never taught you to fight well.

So when conflicts arise—and they will—what do we do? The wife is wondering why *she* has to fix breakfast each morning while her husband sleeps an extra half-hour. When he finally stumbles to the table, he complains that the eggs are too runny. She feels like yelling or crying or breaking an egg on his head, but she doesn't do conflict very well. So what does she do?

She burns his toast.

Some people, like this wife, become masters of *indirect* conflict. They can't bear to have a real fight, so they subtly sabotage their foe. Some couples carry on simmering feuds for years without ever raising their voices. He "accidentally" breaks her favorite vase. She schedules a dinner with friends on the same night as the game he wants to watch. He questions her appearance. She notes the progress of his balding. Round and round it goes in this passive-aggressive nightmare.

Others just *withdraw* from conflict. This passive type just sits and sulks when something is wrong, not wanting to make a big deal of it. The problem is, bad patterns can continue and even grow when one spouse—or both—sits idly. They are successfully avoiding conflict, but soon they may not have much of a marriage.

For those who adopt the *explosive* model, things are quite different. The conflict can escalate quickly—a mild criticism leading to a shouting match. Husband and wife both walk around armed for battle, just waiting for the next hint of disagreement. The problem is that explosive couples soon forget why they're fighting. The actual conflict—the difference of opinion that started the tiff—is never resolved, perhaps never even mentioned. It's about personalities, old wounds, dirty laundry. Just get your punch in before you get knocked out. (This usually happens verbally; but tragically, all too often there are physical punches as well.)

PATTERN RECOGNITION

Think of all the couples that you know well. Can you identify destructive patterns in their marriages? It's pretty easy, isn't it? Many people can see problem areas very clearly in others, but when it comes to their own self-examination, they don't see them (or don't want to face them).

We've developed a simplistic grid that will help you identify possible destructive patterns in your marriage. Certainly the complexities of the interactions cannot be covered in just nine categories, but this approach will help you gain insights into your own unhealthy tendencies. The nine destructive patterns are based on a grid of the three basic *response styles*.

As we have just described, people respond to problems in three basic ways: *aggressive*, *passive-aggressive*, and *passive*. Some *approach* conflict, which is the assertive or aggressive response.

Some *avoid* conflict, which is the passive response. Some *feel* aggression while *acting* passively, which we label the passive-aggressive response.

In order to help you determine how you usually respond, we have developed a simple self-assessment. This is not a scientific test, it is merely presented to provide general insights. Keep in mind that your responses might change according to your moods, so try to answer the way you would normally respond.

Note: You can make a photocopy of this test rather than writing in the book. You'll want to make a second photocopy for your spouse. (Limited permission is granted to photocopy this evaluation for use by you and your spouse in conjunction with your study of *The Marriage Mender.* No pages in any other part of this book may be copied, nor may this evaluation be copied for any other reason.)

RESPONSE STYLE EVALUATION

On a scale of 1 to 5, please rate how strongly the following statements describe your usual response. In this case, 1 signifies "this would not happen" and 5 signifies "this is very likely to happen," while three respresents the possibility that it could happen.

It is important that both husband and wife take the test. (If helpful, you could fill out a second test the way you think your spouse would.)

1. Your spouse criticizes a job you've just done around the house, so you walk away and decide that you'll not do another job for a long time.

    1   2   3   4   5

2. Your spouse criticizes a job you've just done around the house, so you criticize him or her for not appreciating you.

    1   2   3   4   5

(continued on page 148)

(continued from page 147)

3. I tell people what I think even if I know it will be hard for them to hear.

    1   2   3   4   5

4. I say yes to some tasks even though I know I might not get them done.

    1   2   3   4   5

5. When things around me are upsetting, I find a quiet place to calm myself.

    1   2   3   4   5

6. I procrastinate or arrive late when I have to do things that I don't like.

    1   2   3   4   5

7. I tell people what I think they want to hear in order to avoid confrontation.

    1   2   3   4   5

8. When my spouse suggests that we do something that I really don't like, I submit to his or her wishes.

    1   2   3   4   5

9. When I don't like what my spouse is doing, I tell him or her.

    1   2   3   4   5

10. I don't get mad, I get even.

    1   2   3   4   5

11. When my spouse and I disagree, I try to talk him or her into agreement.

    1   2   3   4   5

12. When my spouse and I disagree, I change to accommodate his or her point of view.

    1   2   3   4   5

(continued on page 149)

(continued from page 148)

Add your scores for the following question combinations:
Questions 2, 3, 9, 11
(Aggressive Response)—Total_____

Questions 4, 6, 7, 10
(Passive-Aggressive Response)—Total_____

Questions 1, 5, 8, 12
(Passive Response)—Total_____

What is your most likely response style?

What is your spouse's most likely response style?

COMMON CONFLICT PATTERNS

Certainly there are other variations of personality styles, but the passive/aggressive continuum gives us a basic understanding of our *levels of engagement*. How much do we approach or avoid each other, and what are the results?

It gets interesting when we put husbands and wives together with different response styles. For example, particular patterns emerge when one spouse is aggressive and the other is passive.

Take a look at the grid on page 150 in order to determine the destructive pattern you are most likely to use. Once you identify your destructive pattern, you can take measures to break it.

The interactions in the top left of the grid may be categorized as explosive, meaning the couple engages each other in aggressive, angry, and perhaps violent ways. The responses toward the bottom right are avoidance, more peaceful but less intimate.

Remember that a twelve-point self-test is not going to define you with pinpoint accuracy. But you have a general idea of how passive or aggressive you and your spouse are. This grid will help you name some of the problems you're already facing. The rest of this chapter will explain them in more depth.

Don't be surprised if you and your spouse come up with different analyses of your interactions. You may perceive your conflict differently (which may add to the conflict). Consider all the possibilities as you investigate your susceptibility to the following destructive patterns.

W O M A N			
	Aggressive	P-A	Passive
M Aggressive	Fire with Fire	Sabotage	Abuse Submission
A N P-A	Time Bomb	*Exploding* Guerilla Warfare *Avoiding*	Sudden Death
Passive	Nagging Shut Down	Disappointment	Boredom

FIRE WITH FIRE

When an aggressive man is married to an aggressive woman, sparks fly. Both know what they want and how to get it, and their objectives may create conflict. Aggressive people are often angry, shouting and scolding when they don't get their way. With two aggressive partners, the volume level can be very high.

While there is nothing wrong with conflict in a relationship, when it gets out of balance it may become emotionally and even physically destructive. In some cultures, open conflict is common and acceptable, but it can still cause emotional wounds. When marriage partners fight fire with fire, their words sear each other. The relationship is soon about *winning* rather than *loving*. You fight when you're together and fume when you're not. Where is the love, the submission, the "for better, for worse" commitment?

If you find yourself in this kind of relationship, you need to keep your anger in check. Learn ways to disengage when a fight gets out of hand. Practice calling timeouts and other negotiation strategies. Find times of tenderness to balance out your brawls.

SABOTAGE

When an aggressive man is in relationship with a passive-aggressive woman, he might seem to have the upper hand in controlling the marriage, but she is plotting under the surface. The man seeks to engage his wife in conflict, but she tries to avoid the conflict, finding it is easier to go along for now and then find another avenue to get her way. She may get even with him in subtle ways or sabotage all of the things that he is trying to accomplish, even though she might say that she's "all for it."

A good example is found in a husband who has established an aggressive savings plan for the family. He tells everyone, "This is the way it is going to be," and of course his wife agrees to it. But then she runs up bills and sabotages his budget at every turn.

Many Christian marriages fall into this pattern. A strong wife might want to obey the biblical command to submit to her husband, but also exert her own will in the marriage. She may pay lip service to her husband's leadership but find underhanded ways to manipulate him to do things her way—*and she may not even realize she's doing it.*

In the sabotage pattern, the wife needs to be more open about her desires, and the husband must make an effort to draw out his wife's opinions. Whatever is going on under the surface needs to come out in the open so they can develop workable compromises.

The husband needs to follow the biblical directive to "please his wife" (1 Corinthians 7:33) and not just enforce his own agenda. The wife can express her opinions and still act in a spirit of submission.

ABUSE/SUBMISSION

When an aggressive man marries a passive woman, they have a formula for abuse—emotional if not physical. The previous statement doesn't mean that, if your marriage fits into this category, you must be in an abusive situation. It just means that there is a tendency for the relationship to be one-sided, and in the extreme it can lead to abuse.

Earlier we met Chuck and Lois—the aggressive leader and the submissive wife. It's a common arrangement; these opposites often attract. Their marriage started out fine, but soon everything began to tilt toward Chuck. He made all the decisions and, in her passivity, Lois sweetly agreed. Then Chuck began to abuse Lois verbally, criticizing her in public. Soon he was tearing her down emotionally, comparing her to other women.

Again, this arrangement doesn't have to lead in that direction, but spouses need to be careful. Chuck should have put limits on his tendency to dominate, and Lois needed to speak up when things got out of balance. Unfortunately, they got themselves into a downward spiral. The abuse made Lois shrink into *more* passivity, which Chuck saw as weakness. That made him more angry, which made him berate her all the more. It was all Lois could do to break out of that situation and see a counselor.

But many times, women like Lois just submit in order to avoid conflict, and men like Chuck learn that they can get away with control and manipulation. Some would say this is the biblical model, but it's not. When Chuck scolded Lois as if she were a little girl, he was not loving his wife "as Christ loved the church and gave himself up for her" (Ephesians 5:25). Scripture is full of nonpassive women, such as Priscilla, Lydia, Martha, Esther, and Deborah, who spoke up in a male-dominated world.

To break this pattern, the aggressive husband must work especially hard at understanding the desires of his passive wife. The passive wife must find ways to make her voice heard when she feels strongly about something. She will never learn to like conflict, but she can write a letter, hold a family meeting (for support), or find some other low-confrontation method for making her feelings known.

TIME BOMB

What happens when it's the other way around, when the aggressive one is the woman and the man is passive-aggressive? We call this situation the time bomb, "because you never know when he will explode."

The woman in this type of relationship will constantly engage her husband—ordering him around, nagging him, or just doing things with or without him. On the surface, the husband seems to go along passively with her plans, but he's not happy. He might agree to her list of chores, but then he finds ways to get out of his responsibilities or does them badly.

Some women just submit in order to avoid conflict, and the men in their lives learn that they can get away with control and manipulation. One pattern of coping feeds the other.

In this way, the pattern is similar to sabotage, but the passive-aggressive man is much more likely to blow up at some point. In our culture, and especially in our religious culture, the man who lets his wife wear the pants in the home is considered weak, unmasculine. This creates extra resentment in passive-aggressive husbands, although they still choose not to confront their aggressive wives. Any passive-aggressive person is a pressure-cooker, but this situation turns up the heat. Men seem to be less skilled at subtle manipulation, so they will have less success with under-the-surface ploys than women. In other words, sabotage doesn't work as well for men as for women, so their frustration mounts up until they explode or leave the marriage.

This can be an extremely frustrating situation for the wife as well. She may want her husband to take some leadership, but he continues his avoidance tactics. It may take some work to dig out what he really wants, but that's what the wife needs to do. She needs to empower her husband by stepping back a bit and letting him decide some things—even if he takes too long to decide.

The husband needs to express himself more directly. If he

is unhappy with something, he needs to say so. Both husband and wife need to create safe ways to express their feelings.

GUERRILLA WARFARE

When two passive-aggressives get together, direct battles are avoided. On the surface, both parties try to placate the other, but sabotage is going on from both directions. Bernie and Deb were like that. Bernie was given a list of chores each Saturday morning. He had all weekend to get them done, but every job became a big ordeal. He wouldn't have the right tools, would need to run out to the store for a minute, and would disappear for the afternoon.

When he got home, of course, Deb would be hot. "What happened to you?" she would demand.

Bernie resented having to answer to his wife, but he didn't want to create a fight. He would *feel* like saying, "It's none of your business," or "I decided to go to the golf store and check out some new clubs." But he knew these replies would evoke some wrath, so he lied. "Oh, you wouldn't believe what I went through. The oil light went on in the car, so I stopped at the garage and they said. . . ."

It was hard for Deb to yell at him for that, so she decided to get even in another way. She gave him the cold shoulder all evening, and when he asked her what was wrong, she responded, "Nothing, dear." The next day Deb went shopping and ran up some major charges, because she knew that it would really irk Bernie. They were engaged in guerrilla warfare, even though there was no direct fighting going on.

Passive-aggressive people are the worst negotiators because they simply will not admit there's a problem. They are content to go on for years, hiding their anger and disappointment but subtly making their partners pay. When asked to get the issues out in the open, often they don't even know what the issues are.

Where is the road to health for our passive-aggressive partners? Ironically, they need to learn to fight. They have to be honest about the feelings they've been hiding inside, even if those feelings will create conflict with the other person. (This is a difficult process, one that is probably best to start in a counselor's office.) Each partner needs to draw the other out, calling their bluff and bringing disagreements out in the open where they can be discussed reasonably.

SUDDEN DEATH

When a passive-aggressive man is paired with a passive woman, they can sink into a destructive pattern that we call sudden death. The man may harbor frustrations and disappointments, but he does not express them, since he fears conflict. However, he may be acting out in the relationship—procrastinating, stretching the truth, thwarting her needs, and keeping secrets from her.

The woman doesn't question much and is unaware of how bad the problems might be since, on the surface, the husband is acting as if nothing is wrong.

One day the husband leaves. The wife wonders what happened. In her eyes, the relationship has come to a sudden death, without warning, seemingly without cause.

In such cases, passive women need to be more aggressive, bringing their husbands' feelings out into the open. They must fight their own avoidance tendencies and allow their husbands to express thoughts and feelings, even if those things are painful to hear. The passive-aggressive husbands in these cases must discipline themselves to open up about what bothers them. Vent the steam kettle before it explodes.

Of course, these changes are not easy, but if a couple is committed to improving their relationship, they can develop structures that will help them communicate their feelings—a Friday Night Checkup or a monthly Steam-Venting Talk. A counselor could also help them open up.

SHUT DOWN

When an aggressive woman is married to a passive man, they are susceptible to a destructive pattern in which the man shuts down emotionally. There is more and more separation in the marriage—they may stay together, but they pass like ships in the night.

This was the case with Frank and Nancy, the couple we

considered at the beginning of this chapter. Nancy kept trying to engage Frank, but the more she pushed, the more he shut down. Finally, he totally tuned out of the marriage, living with a Walkman on his ears, and she gave up trying to change the situation. Nancy was frustrated and depressed, and she wanted out.

When it's a passive woman with an aggressive man (as in the abuse/submission pattern above), the woman is usually directed *toward* the relationship. She will stay with her husband no matter what, perhaps even losing her own identity in his. But men are not usually as submissive, even if they are passive. Instead of picking a fight, they'll withdraw. "If I can't be captain, I don't want to play." A man has a basic need for independence that keeps the passive husband directed *away from* the relationship, resisting his wife's attempts to draw him back in.

In such cases, the husband needs to be strongly motivated to reengage with his wife. Sometimes this happens when his wife reempowers him, making him feel important and special. The wife may need to tone down her aggressive pursuit and let him reengage when he's ready. Once she stops chasing him, he may stop running—but this will require patience.

But let's not place the whole burden on the wife. The husband, though he may be passive, has a responsibility to honor his marriage commitment, to "love and cherish" his wife. This requires a turnaround, a decision to become more of an active participant in the marriage.

DISAPPOINTMENT

When a passive-aggressive woman is paired with a passive man, they can sink into a pattern of disappointment. It's possible that they will follow the sudden death pattern, but we find that women are less apt to up and leave a marriage. It's more likely that they'll stay and nurse their frustrations, continuing in an unsatisfying relationship.

In this pattern, the wife tries to make the relationship work, but often finds that she's working alone. Her passive husband has little energy to invest in the relationship, which makes her angry, insecure, and deeply disappointed. But instead of challenging him, she will store up her grievances, until they emerge indirectly, in that acting-out behavior described earlier. It may seem like she's trying to get a rise out of him, but he won't take the bait.

Christian women often find themselves in this pattern. They want their husbands to be the head of the home, but the husbands seem disinterested. They nag and prod and cajole—nothing works. They try manipulation and sabotage and all those other passive-aggressive tricks, and still nothing works. So they live with the disappointment.

Passive husbands have a responsibility to commit themselves more actively to their wives. Whatever else is going on in their lives, they must have energy for their marriages. Passive-aggressive wives need to get their gripes out in the open, but in a manner that stops short of all-out assault. It is healthier for both parties if the issues are shared rather than stuffed. Find an acceptable time for sharing and avoid constant harping (which might make him withdraw more). Perhaps a weekly discussion about the relationship would vent her frustrations while providing some safety for him.

BOREDOM

When two passive people marry, they run the risk of boredom. Both people just get along and keep the peace, avoiding conflict and confrontation. If upset or disappointed about something, they let it go. But over time, avoidance and pulling back can lead to a boring, dead-end relationship. Neither one is learning or growing because there is no challenge to change or work through issues.

In this kind of relationship both parties need to speak up, expressing their needs and feelings more. They should invest more energy in the marriage. Each should actively seek the other's growth.

But then they wouldn't be passive anymore, would they? That's not necessarily true. We're not talking about a thorough personality change, just an ability to halt a destructive pattern. Passive partners must take the risk of talking about the relationship—especially if they find themselves disappointed or bored.

▼ ▼ ▼

These patterns we've discussed are not inevitable just because you have fit a certain square on our grid. Yet they *are* dangers. You can avoid these patterns by practicing good communication, by ensuring each other's safety, and by learning to deal with conflict.

Conflict *will* occur in your marriage. And what do you do when it does? Do you try to win? Do you deny it, but internalize it? Do you avoid it? What does your spouse do?

These are the questions we've been asking in this chapter. What *should* you do with conflict? Read on.

CHANGING YOUR DESTRUCTIVE PATTERNS: SOLUTION-BASED TECHNIQUES FOR BRINGING ABOUT CHANGE

1. *Do something different.*[1] Since what you've been doing isn't working, try something new. If you've been nagging to get attention, try backing off. If you've been distancing yourself and shutting out your spouse, make some new efforts to do things together and share your feelings with each other.
2. *Notice what is different* about the times when the relationship is going well. How do you act? How does your spouse act? What are you doing differently from the times you are in conflict? Begin doing more of that.
3. *Go back in time.* Do you feel as if you're *always* in this destructive pattern? Are you having trouble finding any times when you are not in conflict? Think back to an earlier time in your marriage when things were good. Then do the same analysis.
4. *Notice what you are doing when conflicts start.* Do you have certain times when you're especially vulnerable? Perhaps late at night? After a difficult day? On weekends? Do you have settings that are more troublesome? On vacations? On long car rides? In the kitchen? Determine your most vulnerable times and places and

then prepare for them in advance to avoid destructive behavior.

5. *Identify the triggers* of your destructive patterns. Talk about those triggers and what you might try differently next time. For example, "I start to distance when I perceive that you're trying to control me."

6. *Notice what you did to resolve the problem* when your conflicts end positively—with compromise or agreement. Then make an effort to repeat the pattern in the next crisis.

7. *Who is first to "give the soft answer"* and stop the destructive spiral? You or your spouse? If it's usually you, great! Keep up the good work (and try to be even better at it). If your spouse usually does this, praise him or her for it (and learn how to do it yourself). Both of you should make an effort to be the first to break the destructive pattern. (We're not talking about *avoiding* conflict, but about *controlling* it.)

SOLUTION WORKSHOP SEVEN

GOAL: Identify destructive patterns in your marriage.

If you haven't taken the Response Style Evaluation on pages 147-149, do so now.

1. Based on the Response Style Evaluation, which response style(s) do you generally use?

Husband:

Wife:

2. Consult the grid on page 150, based on your response styles. Which destructive pattern are you most susceptible to?

   Husband:

   Wife:

3. Can you think of a recent incident when this destructive pattern was engaged? What happened?

4. Looking back on it now, what would you do differently?

CHAPTER EIGHT

What *Does* Work:
Moving Toward Healing

Terry and Jean regularly saw their minor arguments escalate into screaming, yelling, and even hitting each other. They met in high school, had an on-again-off-again relationship, and married a few years later. After ten years of marriage, they separated. Yet in a last-ditch effort to save their marriage, they came to me* for counseling.

From their first session, the high level of conflict was obvious. Jean could hardly get a word out before Terry would accuse her of blaming him for the problem.

"He doesn't care about me or respect me," Jean complained. "Once he accused me of having no brains. I think he was serious."

Terry responded with an example of how she had messed up a "simple hotel reservation, which ruined the vacation."

The conflict raged like a battle, with each bringing more reinforcements into the fray. They were still just explaining why they were coming to therapy, and already it was turning into a major fight! Later, after we had established ground rules for communication, both expressed a desire to make the marriage work.

"I care for Terry, I really do," said Jean. "But I don't think he feels the same way about me."

---

*All first person pronouns in this chapter refer to Tom Bartlett.

"I love Jean a lot," said Terry. "But she doesn't seem to return it."

▼　▼　▼

Couples don't fight because they *don't* care about each other, but because they *do*. When people invest themselves in marriage, they begin to fear that they will lose their investment—that they won't get their needs met or that they'll get hurt. These are common, natural fears that lead to common, natural conflicts. Thus *conflict is not something to be avoided in marriage, it is something to be resolved.*

Couples don't fight because they don't care about each other, but because they do.

There's a common thread woven through the destructive patterns we examined in the last chapter: Couples get into trouble when they don't know how to deal with conflict. Whether they try to win all conflicts (aggressive), deny feelings that would lead to conflict (passive-aggressive), or avoid conflict altogether (passive), they settle into harmful habits because they don't know how to fight in an honest, honorable way.

Our competitive culture views all conflict as something to be won or lost—even interpersonal conflict. While some couples get into this mindset, many find it troublesome. Even if you win, your beloved spouse loses. Unless you are a hardened gloater, that's not a satisfactory solution. No wonder so many of us don't approach conflict very well!

Comparing "happy" marriages with "unhappy" marriages, studies have found no significant difference in the *amount* of conflict, but happy couples tend to *handle conflict better.*[1]

CONFLICT QUIZ (TRUE OR FALSE)

T　F　1. Conflict is bad and should be avoided whenever possible.

T　F　2. If my spouse and I truly love each other, we won't have conflict.

T	F	3. Conflict can actually help my spouse and I feel closer.
T	F	4. Before I can resolve conflict with my spouse, I need to feel better about my spouse.
T	F	5. When my spouse and I have a disagreement, we should never get emotional.
T	F	6. Our children should never see us involved in a conflict.
T	F	7. It's better to forget about a conflict (let sleeping dogs lie) than to bring it up later.
T	F	8. All conflicts in our marriage must be completely resolved.

Suggested answers are on pages 177-178.

ACCEPTING CONFLICT

A solution-based approach to your problems must be *realistic*. You will not be able to erase all conflict from your marriage, but you can control it, learn from it, and grow through it. Let's begin by looking at some basic facts.

1. Conflict is a natural phenomenon. If two people are going to live together, they *will* experience conflict. This fact is crucial. We don't have to avoid something good, nor do we have to feel defensive. If we start with an understanding that two partners are allowed to disagree, the stakes are lowered, the conflict deescalates.

2. Conflicts arise out of personal values, beliefs, and needs. No matter how much you love your mate, you are still hot-wired for your own safety and survival. You will seek to meet your own needs, and sometimes the fulfillment of your needs will conflict with the fulfillment of your spouse's needs. This is not necessarily an expression of selfishness — it's a God-given means of survival.

3. Conflicts often emerge as a symptom of a basic underlying need. Jean complained that Terry spent too much time working on his antique car. They argued about how each spent leisure time, but never touched Jean's underlying need—to be close to Terry. When he went to the garage to spend quality time with his car, she felt left out. It was a good, loving instinct on her part, but she expressed it in a nagging way, and he responded in kind.

Conflict is not something to be avoided in marriage, it is something to be resolved.

4. When we don't know how to deal with conflict, we avoid it. You need to see your life together as a training ground. As minor conflicts arise, don't shrug them off. Use them to learn how to resolve conflict. With this practice, you'll be able to weather the major storms when they blow in.

5. Unresolved conflicts are often "gone, but not forgotten." Unresolved conflicts are like weeds. At first they may seem insignificant, not very dangerous to the other plants. But over time they grow and multiply, slowly choking out the life of the flowers. If you wait too long to weed, the weeds cannot be pulled without injuring the flowers.

6. Conflict provides an opportunity for growth. Conflict is like any other type of energy. The power of water can flood and destroy whole towns, yet that same power can be managed in order to provide the benefits of electricity. Conflict in marriage allows a couple to share each other's needs, allowing them to accept and celebrate their differences. Larry Hof of the Marriage Council of Philadelphia defines this as conflict intimacy, describing it as "facing and struggling with differences in such a way that association, connectedness, . . . contact, and warmth are increased."[2]

Therefore, if you "don't do conflict," you really won't have a chance at a close, healthy relationship. Closeness in marriage is only possible when we begin to open up our true feelings to our partner. And that will reveal differences, perhaps even major differences, which lead to some measure of conflict.

When you learn to accept and deal with those differences, you will develop a deeper intimacy in your life together.

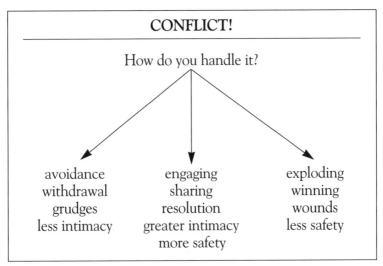

LOOKING BACK

When Terry and Jean came to therapy, each viewed the other as trying to sabotage any attempts at resolving the problems of the marriage. This was a major obstacle to their reconciliation.

Terry thought that Jean was unfeeling and cold. He said she often acted in a condescending manner, issuing pronouncements and then leaving when he reacted to her behavior.

Jean, on the other hand, described Terry as out of control, an emotional roller coaster. Whenever she would try to have a rational discussion with him, she said Terry would raise his voice, argue, or get angry, making it impossible to carry on a reasonable discussion.

We needed to look back into the family history of both Jean and Terry. Perhaps we could find clues to explain their current behavior.

Previous chapters have discussed the solution-based shift in counseling from past-oriented analysis to a future-based hunt for a solution. With Terry and Jean, the goals of therapy were to help them understand their problems, assess what they could do to think or behave differently, and then use tools of communication and conflict resolution to accomplish the changes they desired. Again, all this didn't mean the past was irrelevant. We are all shaped by our past experiences. Understanding our background may help us devise effective strategies for future change.

As we start therapy with couples, we often ask them to write out a brief family history—not to rehash old crises but to decode their present ideas about relationships. The past can explain a lot about a person's behavior. It gives some understanding of the strengths and weaknesses that each one brings to the relationship.

When we discussed safety in chapter four, we examined the importance of intentions. You feel safer when you trust that your spouse does not intend to hurt you. The past can be a window into a person's intentions. If you can see that your spouse received "basic training" which leads him or her to behave in certain ways, then you can begin to understand that behavior as less intentional, less personal. While it may still be annoying or even hurtful, understanding your mate's background may help you react with open communication rather than defensiveness or a counterattack.

I asked Terry and Jean to share a little about their families of origin, specifically how they learned to deal with conflict. As you might have guessed, Jean came from a home where emotions were not expressed. When problems came up, they were dismissed intellectually. She remembered a few occasions when strong emotions were expressed, but they were scary incidents. Loss of control was especially threatening.

Terry grew up in a family where members yelled and argued fairly regularly. A storm would arise, blow over and be forgotten.

As the discussion went on, both Terry and Jean began to understand:

1. They had different training.
2. They approached conflict differently.
3. Both had been operating under the belief that they had been trained in the *right* method.

4. Each saw the other as intentionally attempting to hurt or sabotage the relationship, when that was not the intention.

Once they understood these factors, Terry and Jean became more tolerant of each other. They felt safer and could offer safety by giving the other the benefit of the doubt and being willing to communicate.

GROUND RULES

The answer shouldn't sound magical. It's not as if a therapist waves a magic wand and suddenly the husband and wife get along fine. Terry and Jean *began* to understand each other better. By recognizing their different backgrounds and how those backgrounds shaped their different responses to conflict, they were able to get to square

You feel safer when you trust that your spouse does not intend to hurt you.

one. But conflict management involves a steady process of working together, listening and sharing, and fighting fairly.

How do you get to square two? How do you resolve conflict in the grind of everyday life? Do you need a therapist at home to act as referee?

It might be nice, but it's not necessary. By agreeing to ground rules and developing certain habits in your marriage, you can learn effective conflict resolution. The following principles will get you started:

1. Make it a win-win situation. Instead of trying to win each conflict (at your partner's expense), find a way that both of you can win. Look for ways to use the conflict to improve the relationship. Marriage is not necessarily a zero-sum game. By using your powers of creativity, you can come up with ways to keep you both happy.

2. Find a way to deescalate. Researchers have found that one negative, hurtful comment requires about five positive counteracting comments.[3] When a relationship sustains damage from an insult, it takes five or more compliments to patch things up. That may be a little too quantified for you, but you can probably identify with the basic principle. Everyone enjoys positive feedback, but critical comments stick longer.

When a husband and wife argue, they can quickly start firing those verbal blasts. One follows another as the conflict escalates from conventional warfare to nuclear warfare. Soon they are saying things that cause deep and lasting damage to the relationship.

How can you stop the madness? You have to cool down before things get too hot.

Agree on a gesture or specific phrase indicating that a timeout or break is needed. The "T" sign used for a sports timeout is an optional gesture that is easy to remember. Couples can simply say, "I need a break," or come up with a phrase that has some meaning for them.

Commit to hold that gesture or phrase as sacred. Both spouses recognize it as a serious tool in helping the relationship. Both also agree not to misuse it. In other words, if one spouse is mad at the other and wants to launch a surprise attack, he or she can't sneak in and let the other have it, and then use the timeout to escape.

Whoever calls the timeout is responsible to make a return appointment when he or she will continue the discussion. This helps prevent the surprise attack as noted above and does not allow you to avoid legitimate problems.

3. Accentuate the positive. Think about a teacher or boss in your past that you greatly respected. You probably considered this person fair, even when criticism was given. There was probably a balance of necessary criticism with personal affirmation.

Many of our conflicts are hurtful and unhealthy because we focus on negatives and fail to note the positive things that our mates do. This increases the defensiveness in the relationship, causing us to lapse into our tried and true behaviors. A positive focus does not mean we ignore problems that need to be corrected. But, like that respected teacher or boss did, we need to balance the necessary criticism with positive comments (and remember that 5 to 1 ratio).

You might find it helpful to keep a journal where you list

each day one positive thing your spouse did. Then take the time to let your spouse know that you noticed the action and appreciate it.

4. Use what works. Remember to use this basic premise of solution-based therapy. This sounds obvious, but it's amazing how short our memories can be. Take some time to think about how you have resolved conflicts successfully in the past. Have there been times as a couple that you have been able to disagree without fighting? Together make a list of the things that you and your spouse did that helped you get through the conflict. Then look over your lists together and make a commitment to begin doing what works.

Don't overlook this point just because it sounds so simple. Intelligent couples come to counseling with no clue about resolving their differences. The counselor asks, "Well, have you ever resolved any conflicts in the past? How did you do it? Try that." And they think he's brilliant.

Resolving conflict is not rocket science. Just take a look at the skills you already possess and use them.

5. Stop doing what doesn't work. We humans have a strange habit of continuing to do things that don't do us any good. When the husband comes home late from work, the wife complains about it—and worries to herself that she's beginning to sound like a broken record. But guess what she does the next time he's running late? That's right, she complains again, which is a setup for his same old response, avoidance or anger. And the conflict continues.

Take a hard look at the patterns of behavior getting you into trouble. Determine to stop doing the hurtful things.

Watch out for the triggers too. There probably are specific words or phrases that send you or your spouse into orbit. *Fat, bald, nag, weak, Niagara Falls.* You probably know exactly what they are and what effect they have. You usually save these weapons for the times when a fight gets really rough. Whatever these terms are, take time to identify them with your spouse and agree not to use them in the future.

6. Keep the big picture in sight. We tend to be fairly short term in our approach to progress. As improvements occur, the yardstick by which we measure progress seems to get longer so that we notice our shortcomings without noting the progress. This can lead to greater conflict, just when things are actually going better. It's a case of "not seeing the forest for the trees." Step back. Get the big picture of where you have been and where you're headed. Try to gain a realistic perspective on the progress you have made.

Jean and Terry are typical of many couples who come to therapy with little hope. But after a few sessions of counseling, they began to show improvement. They found that their arguments were not as hurtful or intense, they could communicate, and they had begun to feel closer than they had thought possible just a few weeks earlier.

However, the week after they noted these improvements, they came to their session deeply distressed. They'd had a fight. "It felt like we were back at square one," Terry said. This feeling made him more tense and reactive to Jean, setting up an atmosphere for more conflict.

They needed to review where they had been and how far they had come. I reminded them of the frequency, intensity, and persistent nature of their conflicts when they first came to therapy. "Could you imagine having only one serious argument in a week when you first came in?" I asked. "Did you ever think that you would be able to talk about the things that bother you without it always ending up in a fight?" As they looked at the big picture, they were able to see the amazing progress they had made. This helped them to affirm each other and continue the positive changes they had started.

The *growing yardstick* is a problem often seen in therapy. As things get better, your standards get higher, so you think you're doing worse. Step back. See where you have come from.

7. It takes time. As with any new skill, you need to practice. A piano student will not play a Bach prelude after one lesson. You must set aside time to practice with your spouse. We recommend that you actually schedule at least half an hour (preferably one hour) two or three times a week to develop your communication and conflict resolution skills.

Of course, you don't start out with the hardest task to master, you start with the basics. In other words, practice resolving minor disagreements. Tackle the most volatile issues after you're more seasoned.

It took you a long time to develop the bad habits you have used in conflicts, and it's going to take some time to break the old and learn the new. You will probably lapse back into old habits a few times. Don't be too discouraged by your own lapses, and don't be too hard on your spouse when he or she slips back. Just resolve to do better. Encourage each other as you develop your new skills.

GRATE EXPECTATIONS

Long ago, psychologists identified the significance of expectations on our relationships. Expectations influence our perception of events, our thoughts, and our actions—in marriage, racial prejudice, even choices about moral behavior. Expectations often lead to self-fulfilling prophecies.

In an experiment, teachers were given inaccurate information about the academic abilities and intelligence of new students. In general, the students performed according to the false expectations of the teacher rather than their actual abilities. What the teacher expected of the student subtly influenced how the teacher taught the student, challenged the student, tested the student—and it eventually affected what the student learned.

What does this have to do with marriage? What you expect from your spouse will often be what you receive. If you expect to be hurt, you will act defensively toward your spouse, which will probably hurt your spouse, who may lash back to hurt you. "Aha!" you will say. "I knew I was going to get hurt." But it was your own expectation that set this chain of events in motion.

So what should we do with our expectations? Should we forget about the future and focus only on the present? Is that even possible? Should we always assume the best about everyone, even if that keeps us from protecting ourselves from the worst?

No. We have been created with amazing brains that store and interpret a lot of information. Some of this information helps us anticipate how others in our lives *might* behave — helpful information when used properly. It can help us avoid danger and pain, which is good. I don't know about you, but I don't want to walk into a situation where I have been hurt in the past without a brain that will warn me to be wary.

When a salesman calls offering a time-share in some Caribbean mansion, I expect that he will be smooth-talking and convincing, but totally untruthful. That expectation empowers me to put up my defenses and hang up before I agree to something stupid.

But marriage is different. There can be pain in marriage, but there can also be great blessing. If we anticipate only pain, we can tip the balance and overlook the blessings. We need to take the information our brain gathers and use it constructively. Let's see how this constructive expectation might work:

1. The brain recognizes circumstances which in the past have led to hurt. ("I am going to be late getting home and my spouse will be upset.")
2. You begin to react with an instinctive fight-or-flight response. ("Why can't my spouse greet me nicely? It makes me not want to come home! Maybe I can avoid him or her if I stop at the store and come home even later.") So far, the expectations are beginning to wreak their usual havoc. But here's where you need to make a change. Combat the fight-or-flight instinct with a more rational, constructive approach.
3. You pause to recognize that:
   a. You are arguing in your head with an absent spouse, without really knowing that you're right.
   b. You are making yourself angry in response to your spouse's *imagined* response. (It's your anger rather than your lateness that may cause you and your spouse to argue.)
4. You decide that your brain has alerted you to a potential problem, but you are not powerless to change the situation. You can choose to give your spouse the benefit of the doubt.

5. Your expectation has changed from the inevitability of conflict to the expectation that this is the kind of situation that *can* cause conflict, but you can still do something to change it.
6. You take your spouse's perspective and begin to understand why he or she might be upset. (Your spouse wants to see you, worries about you, has been doing household tasks or child-tending on his or her own, has a meal ready, and so forth.)
7. You walk in the door with a pleasant greeting, acknowledge your spouse's disappointment, and apologize for being late.

So far, so good. But here comes the hard part. Your spouse might respond, at first, just as you had originally expected, complaining angrily about how inconsiderate you are. How do you handle that?

Remember, this is a dance and both of you need to learn the new steps. You are going to step on each other's toes for a while, but you can't stop dancing. You're just not quite synchronized yet.

You have another choice here. You can quickly drop back to the old dance, firing back a zinger, or you can keep working at the new dance and try to lead your spouse in the new steps. In the next chapter, we will outline some of the specific ways to help each other with these steps.

Conflict. It's natural and a normal part of any healthy human relationship. Instead of building walls of avoidance or launching counterattacks, we need to learn how to manage conflict in ways that bring greater intimacy.

SOLUTION WORKSHOP EIGHT

GOAL: Find healthy ways to handle conflict.

Exercise One: Using What Works; Losing What Doesn't
In the left column on the next page, list the two or three most common things your spouse does that irritate you or lead to conflict.

In the middle column, write down the typical way(s) you react when he or she does each of the things you listed. Include little remarks you might make or gestures you might use. (Though these may not seem significant to you, they may be just the thing to which your spouse counterreacts.)

At the right, indicate whether your reaction had a positive or negative (+ or –) effect on your spouse. Positive effects might include a needed change in behavior, enhanced understanding of your feelings, and a greater desire to work with you to improve the situation. Negative effects, of course, include escalation of conflict and avoidance of communication. You might want to create a chart like this in your journal.

CONFLICT STARTER	YOUR REACTION	EFFECT +/–
1.		
2.		
3.		

Now make a decision to practice doing the things that work, those you have marked with a (+). Drop those marked with (–) from your repertoire. Don't expect instant changes, but with some time and patience, changes will occur.

Exercise Two: Writing New Scripts

Review the goals listed below. If the goal is a valuable one for your relationship, fill in the lines below it. Under *Old Way* write a sentence that you might have said in the past—a sentence that would have *escalated* a conflict or *avoided* it in an unhealthy way. Under *New Way* write a revised sentence, one that will help you handle conflict better.

1. Take constructive criticism, rather than internalizing your spouse's suggestions and getting deeply insulted at any comment.
   Old Way:

   New Way:

2. Share emotions rather than holding them in.
   Old Way:

   New Way:

3. Make suggestions rather than blaming.
   Old Way:

   New Way:

4. Use *I statements* when describing your feelings.
   Old Way:

   New Way:

5. Avoid exaggerations such as "you never" or "you always."
   Old Way:

   New Way:

6. Make your spouse feel valued rather than tearing him or her down.
   Old Way:

   New Way:

7. Allow your spouse to have views that differ from yours.
   Old Way:

   New Way:

8. Let go of the need to change or manipulate your spouse.
   Old Way:

   New Way:

Exercise Three: Timeout Policy

During a period of relative calm, talk with your spouse about keeping arguments from escalating or getting hurtful.

Either here or in your journal, fill in the blanks on the following contract according to your individual needs.

TIMEOUT CONTRACT

Both of us desire to decrease the level of conflict in our marriage by talking about problems in a healthy manner and keeping conflict from escalating to the point of being hurtful. In order to accomplish this, we both agree to allow the other to use the timeout procedure we have established.

TIMEOUT GESTURE:
(Example: T sign)

TIMEOUT PHRASE:
(Example: "I'm upset, I need a timeout")

We agree to use these only when truly needed for our mutual benefit and not just to escape from a losing situation.

We agree that whoever calls for the timeout will state a specific time for us to come back together to continue the discussion.

Signed:

Signed:

Date:

ANSWERS AND EXPLANATIONS FOR CONFLICT QUIZ
(see pages 162-163)

1. "Conflict is bad and should be avoided whenever possible." False. In the extreme, conflict can be damaging, but in moderation, conflict can strengthen a marriage.

2. "If my spouse and I truly love each other, we won't have conflict." False. Love will help you work through your conflicts in respectful, healthy ways, but it will not prevent all conflict from happening.

3. "Conflict can actually help my spouse and I feel closer." True. As you express your wants and opinions, you feel more at home in your marriage—even if there is conflict, as long as the conflict is handled in a respectful way.

4. "Before I can resolve conflict with my spouse, I need to feel better about my spouse." False, but it's still a good idea to feel better about your spouse. It is possible to come to an agreement over certain issues even if you remain angry, disappointed, or hurt. But you should address those feelings eventually.

5. "When my spouse and I have a disagreement, we should never get emotional." False, but be careful. Emotions are part of who you are. *Of course*, they will enter into your conflicts. But sometimes emotions can take over your whole way of thinking. Watch out for this. Balance your feelings with good logic.

6. "Our children should never see us involved in a conflict." False. It is beneficial for children to see *more* conflict that is resolved in healthy, loving ways. Children need to learn how to handle conflict well, and they learn best from their parents' modeling.

7. "It's better to forget about a conflict (let sleeping dogs lie) than to bring it up later." False, in most cases. Those sleeping dogs can suddenly attack you at some later point. If it's a genuine, serious issue, talk about it. In fact, it might be better to do so when you're *not* in the heat of the moment.

8. "All conflicts in our marriage must be completely resolved." True and false. It depends on what you mean by "completely resolved." Many issues will remain, say, 80 percent

resolved—and that's fine! This or that little thing may still bother you, but you can live with it. Conflicts do, however, need to be resolved to the point of clearing them out of your way. You need to be able to continue to grow together, without a major disagreement standing between you.

▼ ▼

Moving to Win-Win: Negotiation

Just a few hours before writing this, I* was meeting with a couple in crisis. Aaron and Denise sought counseling because they were dissatisfied with their relationship—and were even discussing separation.

In the past two years, career demands had pulled them apart, allowing less time for their marriage. When they recognized this, they decided to work on their relationship. Aaron, in line with his personality, took the lead, establishing a plan and target date for them to be back on track. This was the solution, as he saw it. When Denise waffled on some of the details, he just reemphasized how important the plan was, which led Denise to feel more anxious and pressured about the relationship. A conflict-avoider, she suggested, "Maybe we should be apart for a while."

Aaron was angry and hurt. "If that's what you want," he replied, "maybe we should just forget about this marriage."

All this happened before they came to see me.

As they told their story, I was struck by their extreme polarization. Aaron had adopted a strict either/or position—"my way or the highway." He was convinced that if Denise would not agree to his plan, she must not care about saving the marriage.

*All first person pronouns in this chapter refer to Tom Bartlett.

Denise was also locked into a black and white view of their situation, especially regarding conflict. Since they couldn't agree on what to do, she felt it was too difficult to do anything.

Ironically, their attempts to fix their relationship just drove them further apart. Although they wanted to save their marriage, both felt unaffirmed, unsafe, alone. From their threatened positions, they started acting defensively, which threatened the other even more.

As we explored this situation further in my office, we learned that Denise actually had other ideas to improve the marriage—she was not sold on separation—but she was afraid of Aaron's reaction to them. Aaron was also willing to be more flexible, but now he felt that Denise was not serious about working on the relationship. The remainder of the session was spent helping them move off their extreme either/or positions to find some middle ground.

GETTING UNSTUCK

In the last chapter we looked at conflict as a natural and normal phenomenon—something to be expected in any intimate relationship. We also examined ways to begin changing the dance of the relationship so that conflicts are less likely to occur and are not as intense when they do occur. We discussed ways of deescalating conflict so that effective problem solving can take place.

But often people get stuck. Aaron and Denise locked into a misunderstanding, and it almost wrecked them. In many cases, misunderstandings can be prevented with good communication skills, a solution-oriented approach to problems, and a mutual commitment to making the marriage safe. Conflict is like a dark tunnel—you don't know for sure what's at the other end. It's a big risk to enter that tunnel, to be honest about your feelings and desires, to engage in a difference of opinion with your spouse. In order to take the risk, you need to have some sense that your partner is committed to working things out, to offering safety, to staying with the conflict long enough to come out the other side of the tunnel with you.

But what do you do when you get stuck in the tunnel, when misunderstandings create an impasse? The key to getting unstuck is good *negotiation*. As Aaron and Denise discovered, you need to put aside your black-or-white thinking and adopt some gray-area compromises.

TRUTH AND COMPROMISES

Unfortunately, many Christians develop such a rigid under-standing of *truth* that they never learn to negotiate the gray areas. Our faith is based on the absolute truth of God's revelation. Justification by faith, the deity of Christ, the love and holiness of God—these are, of course, non-negotiable. But sometimes Christians begin to look for the biblical position on every issue, assuming that there is only one *right* way to think about anything—from how to dress for church to how to scramble eggs.

Misunderstandings can be prevented with good communication skills, a solution-oriented approach to problems, and a mutual commitment to making the marriage safe.

Well, egg-scrambling may be a little extreme. The point is that we are so used to thinking about right and wrong that we don't see the possibility of middle ground. Don't get me wrong: I will fight for the absolute truth of the basics of our faith, but I also believe that God allows for individual expression about understanding many issues of faith and life.

Beware the yeast of the Pharisees. The religious scholars of Jesus' day expanded their understanding of God's law to include a host of human traditions, which they held with a ruthless tenacity. No compromise. Not even when Jesus used the Sabbath day to heal people. He was breaking their law, and thus He was "wrong." But as Jesus said forcefully, they were setting aside God's law in favor of their own invented standards of right and wrong.

Only rarely have I found Christian couples to be at odds

about some clear biblical truth, but I regularly find couples digging trenches around personal opinions or values.

- ▾ A woman can't imagine going to any church other than the one she grew up in, even though her husband doesn't feel at home there.
- ▾ A man thinks it's biblically ordained that he should balance the couple's checkbook, even though his wife is the better accountant.
- ▾ A woman refuses to let her teenage daughter go to school dances, since she was raised to believe dancing is worldly behavior. Her husband has no such qualms.
- ▾ A Republican man is shocked to learn that his wife voted for a Democratic candidate.
- ▾ A woman thinks that it's part of a husband's divine mandate to take out the trash since her father always did.
- ▾ A man assumes that it's part of a wife's divine mandate to cook dinner every night even though his wife works full time and gets home later than he does.

Healthy conflict resolution requires the ability to realize that almost everything can be seen from more than one perspective. Sure, there are a few nonnegotiables, but there are many issues that *must* be negotiated if a couple has a major disagreement. Otherwise they are doomed to a polarized marriage.

Healthy conflict resolution requires the ability to realize that almost everything can be seen from more than one perspective.

In the case of Aaron and Denise, each was viewing his or her own position as the *right* one. They were unable to work on reconciliation until each was willing to see that other opinions were valid and worthy of at least legitimate consideration.

It's crucial to keep the flow of ideas and alternatives going. No one but God has all the answers. In our search to find solutions, this book might have part of the answer and you might have another part. If we can allow for an exchange of ideas, we increase our chances of finding something that works.

Do's and Don'ts
Consider a few general tips for negotiation and conflict resolution.[1]

Do
1. Pick a *specific time* to discuss the problem, a time that works for both of you.
2. Remind yourself and each other that you want this to be a *win-win situation*. It's not his or her problem—it is a problem that we need to resolve.
3. Start with a minor problem that has a good chance of being resolved. *Practice* with easier concerns will improve your skills for the time when bigger problems or impasses need to be tackled.
4. Remember that the goal is to *find a solution*—one you both can live with, not necessarily your first choice.
5. *Stay in the present.* If you can solve the problem that you are experiencing at the present time, that's a win. Reaching back into the past rarely helps solve a problem. The past has relevance—but usually only when it is used as a way of defining the problem and the behavior change being requested.
6. *Stick with one topic.* Make a commitment to go as far as you can on one issue before moving on to the next.[2] Most escalation occurs because couples don't stay focused on the topic and allow skirmishes to break out all over the place—any of which could erupt into a war.
7. Practice the *communication skills* from chapter 6.
8. Use a *time out* when needed. You are better off to call a time out early (following the rules from chapter 6) than to wait until tempers flair.
9. *Fight the temptation to duck the conflict.* While both men and women can be avoiders, men tend to do so more. Hang in there.

DON'T
1. *No sarcasm.* This is an invaluable rule. After all your work to make the relationship safer, nothing breaks it down faster than sarcasm.
2. *No name calling.* This shuts down communication. It's okay to describe behavior and take responsibility for how you feel about it *(I messages)*, but name calling is an attack and only serves to start the defensive reaction cycle.

HOW TO NEGOTIATE

Effective negotiation follows several well-defined steps. Most of this is common sense—you may be doing it already. But if you get stuck, you may want to review these components of conflict resolution.

1. Recognize the problem. You have to admit there is a problem. It's always surprising how long couples ignore, put off, or deny that they are experiencing a significant problem in their marriage. To solve a problem we need to acknowledge that it exists and begin identifing our feelings about it.

2. Decide to practice Christian submission. In Ephesians 5, the Apostle Paul teaches about marriage. You are probably familiar with the injunctions for wives to submit to their husbands and for husbands to love their wives with the totality of Christ's love for us. That section can be summed up by the introductory verse: "Submit to one another out of reverence for Christ" (Ephesians 5:21).

When you experience relational conflict, it is critical to focus on the ultimate goal: *Your marriage relationship should be glorifying to God; it should present a picture of the redemptive work of Jesus Christ.*

God asks us to submit to one another. So, as you consider conflict resolution, remember to ask yourself which is more important—*winning the argument* or *restoring your relationship*? As long as you maintain an attitude of "I'm right, my partner's wrong, I have to win this fight," you will not get very far. But if, right at the start, you adopt the attitude of servanthood and submission that Christ modeled for all believers, your conflict resolution will be much easier. This doesn't mean you avoid the issues. It doesn't mean you stuff your true feelings. It just means you've decided that love is more important than winning—and this attitude will affect all the decisions you're about to make.

3. Translate feelings into recognizable behaviors. One therapist calls this *videotalk.*[3] What does your spouse *do* that' bothers you? Be specific. It does no good to identify a problem or your feelings about it, if you cannot describe it *in terms of behavior* (actions or words). People frequently use adjectives to describe their mates—he's grumpy, she's cold, he's mean, she's disinterested. Use verbs to describe the actual actions involved. That way, your spouse will be able to identify the problem more easily. For example, if I am to change my "cold" behavior toward you, I need to know what I do that gives you the idea that I am cold toward you. (Remember the nonverbal signals we all send out? Those subtle—and sometimes not so subtle—behaviors or signals that accompany and give the full meaning of what we are attempting to communicate, that's what we're identifying here.)

In the previous chapter, I mentioned Terry, who said that he was tired of being put down by Jean, and would like her to respect him. It was hard for her to grasp what he wanted. However, when asked to specify his complaint in the form of a specific behavior, he was able to say, "Whenever I offer my opinion in a group, you sigh." Much better! Now if Jean wants to improve her relationship with Terry, she has something clear and specific to work on. She knows what to change.

This crucial step of conflict resolution involves moving beyond feelings, formulating a specific definition of the problem.

4. Get feedback. Check with your spouse to see how he or she sees the problem. Attempt to understand your spouse's point of view, and acknowledge his or her feelings.

5. Identify any common areas of agreement. This might be as simple as agreeing that a change is needed, but it helps you see that agreement *is* possible. (It can also provide a humorous moment even when there is a high degree of conflict.

Frequently the first time that a couple smiles at each other in a therapy session is when they are able to make a joke about how little they agree on. They agree that they're disagreeing, but it's a start.)

6. Brainstorm solutions. This is probably one of the most important aspects of conflict resolution. As noted previously, we tend to think in terms of *right and wrong* when it comes to relationships, even when the issues have little to do with the truths of Scripture. Brainstorming helps develop alternatives instead of staying stuck in a right versus wrong (my way versus your way) pattern of thinking.

In brainstorming, both partners express any ideas they have about solving the problem—*without criticism or comment from each other.* Allow creative juices to flow; no idea is too wacky. Often a ridiculous idea will turn out to be helpful in the long run. Even if it's too unrealistic to put into practice, it can be the catalyst to free up other ideas that are more workable. One partner should take responsibility to jot down the ideas, but both must resist the temptation to evaluate the options. That will come later.

7. Forecast the consequences of your brainstorming ideas. Now you can evaluate the ideas generated by brainstorming. Look at the potential outcomes of each, noting the positive and negative aspects of every potential course of action. Each of you will probably prefer a different solution, but at least you have several to choose from. Look at them from your spouse's perspective. (This may help you tweak some of the ideas to achieve an acceptable compromise.)

8. Choose a course of action. This can be the most difficult part in the process, the *compromise and agreement stage* of conflict resolution.[4] Go through your brainstorming list and rate each alternative—1 for your first choice, 2 for your second choice, and so on. Your spouse will do the same. Then compare notes. Is there an idea that made the top three on both your lists? The top four?

Remember: The goal of conflict resolution is to find a solution that both of you can agree on, not to have one person *win.* This is where compromise comes in—you are seeking a solution that both of you can live with, although it may not be either of your first choices. (Sometimes, faced with a mediocre compromise solution, couples are motivated to hammer out an alternative that is a combination of both first choices.)

9. *Define the course of action.* Take the time to put the solution into very specific terms, defining each person's responsibility, the specific behavior requested, and ways to communicate if the other doesn't follow through. It is often helpful to establish a short-term goal and set up some future checkpoints for reevaluation. For many behavioral changes, a two-week checkpoint is reasonable. At that time, discuss any problems and make needed adjustments.

10. *Pursue forgiveness.* As you embark on these new measures, take time to ask for forgiveness for any feelings of ill will, bitterness, and for hurtful words or deeds. Be ready to grant forgiveness to your partner for these same offenses. As I said previously, forgiveness doesn't carry with it automatic trust. Forgiveness is granted, but trust is earned. You can choose to let go of the hurt your spouse has caused, while still maintaining healthy boundaries which safely allow you to rebuild trust.

11. *Celebrate.* You have worked hard if you have proceeded through these steps. In any conflict resolution, there is anxiety—a sense of going into that long, dark tunnel and not knowing where it will come out. When you do emerge from the tunnel, you have a reason to celebrate. Go out to dinner, take a mini-vacation, make love—find some way to recognize your success and not taking any easy ways out. You deserve a break.

As a marital therapist, one of the most exciting and rewarding aspects of working with couples is to watch the transformation that occurs when a couple commits to the development of a "win-win" approach to the relationship. People whose relationship was marked by anger and hurt begin to listen to each other's point of view, begin to find ways to come to agreement rather than build walls of distance and defense, and begin to experience the closeness and intimacy that come from being willing to "hang in there" and work through the conflict.

You can experience this transformation toward intimacy. Together with your spouse, commit to a "win-win" approach to relationship conflict. Recognize that conflict is a natural occurrence in any relationship and choose to practice healthy communication, conflict resolution, and negotiation. Admittedly, it takes work, but everything of value does. What could be of greater value than a fulfilling marriage based on mature love?

SOLUTION WORKSHOP NINE

GOAL: Negotiate a resolution to a conflict.

1. Define your view of the conflict issue. Include your feelings and the specific behaviors you see contributing to the problem.

2. Identify your contribution to the problem.

3. Ask your spouse to share his or her view of the problem. What are the areas of agreement?

4. Brainstorm a list of alternatives or potential solutions. Don't worry whether these are good or bad, just start writing ideas!

5. Evaluate each of the alternatives by listing both positive and negative aspects of each, noting your first, second, and third choices.

6. Share your responses (compare answers) with your spouse. Formulate an agreed-upon alternative from among the choices each of you rated as the top three.

Alternative:

My responsibility is:

Your responsibility is:

Date for reevaluation is:

Our celebration for our hard work is:

PART FOUR

Putting Humpty Dumpty Back Together Again

▼ ▼

Forgiveness

F red and Wilma needed help.

Yes, *that* Fred and Wilma. I* was watching Saturday morning cartoons with my kids and found that the Flintstones desperately needed solution-based counseling. Wilma was cleaning a closet when she came upon some of Fred's old memorabilia—bowling trophies, an old football jersey, and things like that. Assuming that Fred hadn't even looked at the stuff in years, she threw the whole box away. When Betty Rubble questioned her decision, Wilma explained, "Oh, he'll never even miss it."

You can guess what happened next. Within a day Fred was invited to get together with some old buddies, and they all decided to wear their old football jerseys. When Fred asked about his box of high school memorabilia, Wilma avoided the issue at first, but then she mused, "Didn't you throw that box out a long time ago, Fred?"

Fred suspected Wilma of trashing his mementoes, but he couldn't prove it. A grudge began to develop. Wilma denied her wrongdoing, but felt guilty, knowing she would have to come clean with Fred at some point. But could Fred ever forgive her for throwing away his stuff—and then lying about it?

In the simplistic 'toon world of television, Wilma was able

*All first person pronouns in this chapter refer to Tom Whiteman.

to retrieve the items in time for a happy ending. But in the real world it seldom works out that well. We knowingly and unknowingly hurt our partners again and again. These hurts tend to put up walls between us, eventually doing serious damage to a relationship—unless a couple can reach a point of forgiveness.

MORE THAN WORDS

Most Christians recognize the value of forgiveness. Our faith is based on the fact that God forgives our sin, and Scripture teaches us to forgive one another. But, frankly, this is a lot harder than it sounds. In any intense relationship (such as marriage), we find our ability to forgive challenged continually.

It may be something as simple as throwing out an old football jersey. Or it may be as serious as an extramarital affair. At any level, forgiveness is tough, and it does us no good to pretend otherwise.

While the solution-based counseling model discounts the value of dwelling on past hurts or jousting about who did what to whom first, we still must face the wrongs done. We can't pretend that a grievance never happened. Even in a solution-oriented approach, we must look at the issues that led up to the problem.

We believe that a biblical model for forgiveness agrees with this focus. We are commanded to ask for forgiveness and also to forgive others, but there is much in Scripture to indicate that wholehearted repentance and restitution are needed too. It is relatively easy to say the words "Please forgive me," but truly *seeking forgiveness* (or granting it) involves more than mere words.

SAFETY REVISITED

Hold up your hand, palm flat out, fingers spread. A safe marriage is like this. Both partners are feeling open, valued, and free to discuss any issue. This is the way we want marriage to feel all of the time, isn't it? Adam and Eve were probably like this before they sinned. "The man and his wife were both naked, and they felt no shame," the Bible tells us (Genesis 2:25), indicating not only their physical closeness, but also their emotional intimacy—naked, no barriers, completely open.

But, as Gary Smalley illustrates in his video series "Hidden Keys to Loving Relationships," an open hand begins to close as we experience hurt, resentment, and brokenness in marriage. And we do experience these things.

So take your open hand and start to draw the fingers together. Start to cup your palm, just a bit. Many of us find ourselves (and our relationships) in this midway position—not completely closed, but also not totally open or safe.

What happens now? When a husband and wife are guarded, partially closed, defensive, they begin to hold back their true feelings. They withhold information that a partner might use against them. Wilma tells Fred that *he* must have thrown out his own stuff. They may still appear to have an open, trusting marriage, but walls are being built. It's hard to apologize for a wrong deed in an atmosphere that we perceive as unsafe.

Take your partially closed hand and slowly—slowly!—close it all the way. This is what often happens to a relationship. You hurt me, I close up, I don't trust you, you get hurt, you lash back at me, I defend myself. The hand closes more with each new difficulty.

What do you have now? A fist.

No one enters marriage expecting a fifteen-round fight. But, as time goes by and hurts adds up, the open hands close into fists. In order to restore safety to the relationship, each person needs to take the chance of opening his or her hand again and extending it to the other person.

This is forgiveness. It takes *time,* a *spirit of humility, courage,* and a lot of *hard work.*

THE WORK OF FORGIVENESS

That's right, forgiveness *is* hard work. Instead of seeking forgiveness, Wilma avoided the issue and even lied about it, building a wall of mistrust between herself and Fred. Obviously she feared his wrath (an indication that the relationship was already partly closed) and decided it was best not to upset him. Maybe the issue would go away.

But those issues do not just go away. Wilma needs to bite the bullet (bite the boulder?), sit Fred down and tell him the truth, offering a sincere apology.

How is Fred likely to respond? If you know anything about this cartoon series, you know he will *not* say, "Oh, that's okay, dear. Don't worry about it." No, you're already hearing him yell, "WIL-MAAAAA!"

Fred will rant and rave about how important that box was, how could she ever do such an ignorant thing, how he will get his revenge, and so on.

Now put yourself in Wilma's sandals (or bare feet). As Fred is yelling at you, you can feel your own spirit beginning to close. You're thinking, "You see, it doesn't pay to be honest with this guy!" It would be quite natural for you to respond with a defensive statement: "Well, if you had clearly marked the box, maybe I would have known to save it!" Or, "If you remember, you lost that ring that my mother gave me, and that had a lot of sentimental value too! But I don't hear you apologizing for that, do I?"

These statements only further close Fred's spirit. You started well with the apology, but a defensive statement now will negate your good start. As the Bible says, "A gentle answer turns away wrath" (Proverbs 15:1). This is the first step in reopening the hand, creating new safety in the relationship. You must sit there, listen to Fred, and *then* respond with something like, "I can tell that I've really wronged and hurt you deeply. Can you forgive me?" That's a spirit-opening statement, and it's very hard to do.

But Fred may not be ready to forgive. Even if Wilma humbly apologizes and asks for forgiveness, Fred may still need time to sulk. He is likely to continue feeling mad—and may even seek to punish her in some way. This is a normal response to his deep hurt. Forgiveness takes time.

FORGIVE AND FORGET?

Forgive and forget. You've heard that phrase a zillion times—the ideal of a restored relationship. But let's take a second look at that concept. Do we really have to become brain-impaired in order to get over some deep hurt?

I don't think we ever really forget a deep hurt. Maybe if it's just a hurtful word or something like Wilma's tossing of Fred's football jersey, eventually we might forget about the incident. But when one partner has an affair, does the other one ever forget it? When one friend betrays another, is that ever forgotten? When one person's addiction robs a whole family of love and trust, is it still a matter of "forgive and forget"?

On a business trip, Art was unfaithful to his wife, Sylvia. Feeling guilty for months afterward, Art finally confessed. They decided to come to me for counseling.

Even before she learned of his infidelity, Sylvia had felt Art distancing himself from her emotionally and physically. She had been worried about the relationship, but when he admitted his affair, she was devastated. At this point, she wasn't sure she wanted to go on living.

This, of course, added to Art's guilt. Both he and Sylvia were in a lot of pain.

What was the real issue here? The infidelity? Maybe. But I sensed there was a deeper wound. Rather than probing the problem deeper, I wanted to focus on a *solution,* so I asked her what would it take to help her feel better. Sylvia responded with two things: "I need to know that Art loves me and still wants me; and I need to know that I can trust him again."

We spent the next several minutes listing all of the ways that Art could reassure her of his love, and then ways in which he could begin to rebuild trust. Art was very motivated to undo the damage he had caused, so he agreed to work on each of the things Sylvia listed.

I then asked Art what it would take for him to feel better. With tears in his eyes he responded, "I know God has forgiven me for what I did, but I need to know that Sylvia forgives me."

They both cried for a brief time, and then Sylvia said, "Yes, Art, I can forgive you." She said it very calmly, but very confidently. She made the *choice* to forgive!

Forgiveness is a choice, a decision to release someone from a debt. You no longer feel like that person owes you, and you decide that you will *not* try to even the score.

As Christians, we should understand this concept better

than most. Our faith rests on the concept of divine forgiveness. I have a debt I cannot pay, but God chose to send His Son to pay the debt for me. Therefore, I have been released from my debt because of God's grace. There is no getting even—God remembers my sins no more.

But can Sylvia afford to *remember Art's sins no more?* Just because Sylvia makes a decision to forgive Art, does that mean the issue is now forgotten or fully resolved? Of course not. There are still many aspects of restoration. Trust needs to be rebuilt. The relationship cannot go back to where it was, at least not for a while. Healing *requires* that they recognize what has occurred and work together to mend the damage. Forgiveness is a process.

> Forgiveness . . .
>> takes a spirit of humility,
>> requires hard work,
>> needs time,
>> requires an open spirit,
>> involves a decision,
>> and is a process.

Sylvia soon discovered that she had been wounded very deeply and was experiencing a type of grieving. Her grieving can last months, even years. In this case, Sylvia really wanted to be done with it. She honestly decided to forgive Art but still found herself crying silently, and even waking up at night with fearful dreams about losing Art to another woman. She worried when he was at work and could not even bear the thought of him going on another business trip.

Had she really forgiven him? And if she had, why were these emotions still plaguing her?

I believe Sylvia *had* forgiven Art, but was still working through the process of forgiveness. You see, there are always consequences to sin. And just because we ask for forgiveness and are forgiven, does not mean there won't be ongoing consequences or sorrow.

In Art and Sylvia's case there were serious consequences for both of them. Art had to check in more often. He avoided all business trips for a while, and when he could not put them off, he only went away for one night. While he was gone, he called his wife about every hour or so to reassure her that everything was okay.

Forgiveness is a decision to release someone from a debt. You no longer feel like that person owes you, and you decide that you will not try to even the score.

Art confided in me privately one day that all the checking in and suspicion on his wife's part were really getting to him. "When will she really forgive me and put this behind us?" he asked.

"I believe she has forgiven you," I responded. "It's just that now you're helping her get over the hurt. You're gradually rebuilding the trust that was broken."

For about a year Art walked on eggshells, and Sylvia gradually started feeling more love and trust for her husband. Her spirit was slowly opening like a clenched hand returning to the open position. Art knew that he was over a major hurdle when he called in from a trip and Sylvia kindly acknowledged that he really didn't need to check in so often.

About a year later I saw Sylvia briefly. We exchanged pleasantries and then I asked her how her marriage was going. She said, "You know, it's like it wasn't even Art who hurt me two years ago. It's a new and different Art that I'm married to now. We have a much better relationship today than we ever had before. I certainly wouldn't recommend that anyone go through what we went through, but I'm glad for the changes that this has brought into our marriage."

Forgiveness takes time. You must first open your heart and your spirit to the other person. Then make the hard choice to forgive, relieving the person of any need to grovel or do penance. But the hard work of restoration is just beginning. You both must choose to learn and grow from the experience. This process includes grieving some losses, learning how to move forward in a healthy new lifestyle, and choosing an attitude of forgiveness every time the feelings of resentment and anger begin to creep up again. Over time God does bring healing, but not unless you *choose* to forgive the one who wronged you, and prayerfully consider what you can learn from the experience.

WHY REMEMBER A HURT?

1. To reflect on what we might want to change about ourselves.
2. To recognize how far God has brought us, and where we might be now in the healing process.
3. To pray for those who hurt us.
4. To help us work through future hurts and perhaps our own wrongdoing.

AIN'T TOO PROUD TO BEG?

What do you do if you're the one who has done the wrong? You have acknowledged your error, but the other person won't forgive you. Or they say they forgive you, but act like they're still trying to even the score? Do you have to keep asking for forgiveness? Do you need to beg?

These are tough questions. Most marriages deal with this problem at some point. It's relatively easy to restore a relationship when both partners are willing—one willing to seek forgiveness and the other willing to forgive. But when the wronged partner is unforgiving, what can the guilty partner do?

First, remember the closed hand. The unforgiving partner has probably closed his or her spirit to you, and you need to find ways of reopening it. You can't do that by yelling, warning, shaming, or threatening. "You call yourself a Christian? You have to forgive me or I'll tell everyone at church what you're really like!"

Will that help to open anyone's spirit? Of course not. The fist will just tighten further.

You do not want to go on the offensive in this situation. Remember your position. You have done wrong. You have caused pain. You are now asking a favor. Even if you are both Christians, forgiveness cannot be demanded. Your partner does not owe it to you. You are asking your partner to take a chance on you, a chance of being hurt again. Your partner has every right to have a closed spirit. Now, is there any way to coax it open?

The first attempt is the apology, which you have already offered. Was it sincere? Did you recognize the full extent of your misdeeds? Was it unconditional?

Let's go back to the example of Wilma. Let's say her apology went something like this: "I'm sorry I threw away your stuff, but you really needed to get rid of it anyway."

That's what we call a *conditional apology*. These usually contain a *yeah-but* clause in them. If there was any excuse or *but* in your apology, then go back and apologize more sincerely.

Or you may have used *blame shifting* in your apology. Kids are especially good at this technique: "I know you told me not to go in the water, but Joey pushed me." (That's one I used as a kid.) Even adults use this technique at times: "I know I said I'd be home by 6:00, but my boss wanted me to. . . ."

While Joey or the boss may have affected your behavior, you still need to take full responsibility for the wrong you committed. "My boss asked me to stay and finish payroll, but I know you told me that you had a doctor's appointment at 6:00, so I should have called or gotten someone else to fill in for me. I was wrong to come home late today. I know that it really messed up your day, and you have good reason for being angry with me. I hope that you will be able to forgive me."

HOW TO APOLOGIZE
1. Confess honestly your wrongdoing and fully accept responsibility.
2. Offer no excuse and do not attempt to shift the blame.
3. Acknowledge the level of hurt and pain that you have caused.
4. Verbalize your remorse and desire to be forgiven.
5. Demonstrate signs of repentance, such as changed attitudes and behaviors.

Conditions, excuses, and blame shifting are manipulative. They erode trust rather than restore it.

But what if this has all happened before? You are late for the umpteenth time. If it's not your boss, it's the train or the traffic or the terrorist incident that happened on your way home. You have become adept at apologizing with so much practice.

Do you wonder why you're not being forgiven? Apologies can lose their effect, after about the tenth or twentieth time. Your partner may be withholding forgiveness because he or she does not trust what you're saying. That's why our apologies need to be followed by an attitude or behavioral change. In religious terms, you might call this *repentance*. You stop the offensive behavior, confess it, and then turn the other way.

This step—repentance—may require some time to demonstrate that you really have changed, such as when Art had to prove to Sylvia that he really could be trusted again. Will your partner's spirit reopen to you? Maybe. Your only remaining tools are prayer, patience, and persistence.

▼ *Prayer*
Pray that God will open your partner's spirit, and that He will give you the strength and wisdom to know how to respond.

▼ *Patience*
When you're trying to mend fences and your partner is stonewalling, the natural, human reaction is to get mad and resentful. You need patience to continue being nice when you're getting little or no reinforcement.

▼ *Persistence*
Don't continue to apologize, as long as you have done so sincerely. But you do need to persist in your attempts to demonstrate love, concern, and the desire to improve the relationship. This can be done by reassuring hugs, persistent nonsexual touch, and

affirming words of encouragement—even if your partner is not as receptive as you'd like.

What if Sylvia didn't accept Art's apology? What if she was cold and closed to him for several months? What could Art do to help her forgive him?

First, he could pray that God would open her spirit. If Sylvia was willing, they could even pray together.

Then Art would need to show patience, treating her gently and lovingly. He would need to make behavioral changes in order to rebuild trust. (We already discussed some of these.) But he would also need to make *spirit-opening* gestures as well. He wouldn't want to do this in a manipulative way: "Oh, I'll buy her some flowers and gifts and she'll get over it eventually." Instead he might discuss how he knows that he's hurt her deeply but that he's committed to rebuilding the relationship. He might even ask her to give him hand signals from day to day, showing how open or closed her spirit is toward him—a closed fist, a partially open fist, and then a hand which is steadily opening.

> *An apology must be followed by attitude and behavior changes which verify that the apology was sincere.*

In a solution-based model, we would ask, "How did Art win Sylvia's trust during the very beginning of their relationship?" While they were dating, Art paid close attention to her needs, listened to her ideas and concerns, and sent her little cards and notes. They went on special dates, held hands, and exchanged reassuring hugs and kisses. *Now Art needs to do all those things that he did to win her over in the beginning.*

FORGIVING OURSELVES

Sometimes in relationships, wrongdoers repent and are forgiven—but a problem remains. There are times when people don't forgive *themselves* for making mistakes. Apologies are sincerely proffered, but they keep beating themselves up over the mistakes. They obsess about what they did wrong, unable to get beyond the failure. This can be a sign of depression or a low self-image. Those who feel that they deserve to be punished will sometimes continue to punish themselves long after God and others have forgiven them. Their feelings of guilt can be frustrating and even debilitating in their relationships.

If you are a person who has a hard time forgiving yourself, or if you struggle with excessive guilt, you need to seek help for yourself in overcoming these feelings.

I'VE HAD ENOUGH!

Are there times when we shouldn't forgive? When hurts or wrongdoing are chronic and deep, you may find yourself in the position of wondering whether you should forgive at all.

Doing Fresh Start divorce recovery seminars around the country, I run into this question all the time. People are dealing with hurts that go well beyond their human ability to forgive. "Why should I forgive him?" I'll hear. "He'll just think that what he did was okay. Maybe if I don't forgive him, it'll teach him a lesson."

Those who feel that they deserve to be punished will sometimes continue to punish themselves long after God and others have forgiven them.

Certainly God wants us to forgive and be reconciled, even when the wounds are deep. But there are some legitimate parameters regarding how we do this.

A woman stalked up to me angrily after I had spoken about forgiveness at a seminar for separated and divorced people. "You Christians are all alike," she ranted. "You judge me and tell me what I should do, but you don't have to live in my shoes!"

"Back up," I begged. "What do you think you heard me say?"

"You told me that I needed to forgive my husband and be reconciled. But he was abusive to me for years. I took the abuse far too long because my pastor told me I should submit. Then when I saw him begin to abuse my children as well, I gathered the courage to leave him for good. Now you tell me I have to forgive him as if it never happened."

I thanked this woman for coming to me immediately and not walking away with a misconception; I needed to clarify some things. When wrongdoing is chronic, reconciliation is difficult and perhaps inadvisable.

We can forgive within our spirits, but the full restoration of a relationship requires the commitment of both parties. Forgiveness means that we don't harbor ill will toward the person who wronged us, but it does not mean that the wrong was right.

Here's a trivial but helpful example. I have a friend who is always late. Before I knew this about him, I offered to carpool with him to church on Sunday mornings. The first time he was to pick me up, he arrived about a half hour late, making us a half hour late to church. Well, I'm one of those people who really wants to be on time, or even early, so I let my friend know how I felt. He apologized and offered to make it up to me by driving the next week, promising to be early.

As you might guess, he was a half hour late again but apologizing profusely, promising that he'd never let it happen again. He even offered to come *an hour early* the next week and treat me to breakfast at a diner on the way to church.

Not only did we miss breakfast the next week, but we were late to church again.

Do I need to forgive my friend for being late? Yes. I need to accept his sincere apology. I should not let his chronic tardiness destroy our friendship. He feels terrible about this, and I should release him from his debt to me. Yes, he made me late to church a few times, but that cannot be undone. I choose not to hold a grudge against him, which would only wreck a relationship and poison my spirit.

But will I let him pick me up for church next week? No, thank you. I'll drive myself to church.

So it is in marriage, when there is chronic abuse, lying, or affairs. Wronged partners need to get to a point of forgiving their spouses, but they should also take steps to get out of the position where they can be hurt deeply again.

As a Christian, I believe wholeheartedly in the sacredness of the marriage commitment. But I also believe that there are times when an abused partner must separate himself or herself for protection and perspective. It's a simple issue of safety. If a wife is being physically abused by her husband, she should *move out*—and then work toward reconciliation through counseling. I recommend that an abused spouse not return until there is strong evidence of behavioral changes in the abusive spouse.

When wrongdoing is chronic, reconciliation is difficult and perhaps inadvisable. We can forgive within our spirits, but the full restoration of a relationship requires the commitment of both parties. Forgiveness means that we don't harbor ill will toward the person who wronged us, but it does not mean that the wrong was right.

If your spouse repeatedly has affairs, it is not your Christian duty to ignore the problem, to "forgive and forget." Your errant spouse is violating the marriage commitment, and you need to stand up for those promises you both made. If your partner is truly repentant, you need to work through the forgiveness process together, demanding an end to the infidelity.

How can you tell if your spouse is *truly repentant?* You need more than an apology (although it starts there). Your spouse should take strong steps away from the misbehavior and toward the marriage—cutting off ties with the other person, staying out of tempting situations, agreeing to counseling, committing time and energy to you. If your spouse is not willing to offer these *fruits of repentance*, you should question his or her sincerity and take steps to protect yourself from future infidelities.

If your partner continues to break your marriage vows, you may need to attend to your own safety by putting some distance in the relationship—if not moving out, maybe moving to a different bedroom (especially with the possibility of sexually transmitted diseases). You are still committed to the marriage, but your spouse is flouting that commitment. You are saying, in essence, "Meet me here at the altar of our sacred marriage vows. But if you have no interest in that, I need to look out for my own well-being."

In cases of chronic lying, you may not have grounds to leave the person, but you want to make sure you protect yourself from hurt. You simply cannot trust your spouse's word, so you'll need to rely on others for reality checks. Don't feel guilty for double-checking and verifying the stories of your lying partner. If he or she says, "Would I lie to you?" your appropriate response is, "Yes, you have done so on many occasions, and I can't afford to trust your word anymore." It is hard to maintain a relationship without trust, so you will almost certainly need counseling to restore a healthy relationship.

There are many chronic behaviors that are less damaging, but still annoying. Your spouse may be late or disorganized or forgetful or rude. Good communication is crucial in dealing with such issues. You must let your spouse know how much the offensive behavior hurts you. While you do not expect perfection, you do expect effort, and you hope for improvement.

One problem with a lot of chronic behavior in marriage is that both partners get used to it. The offending spouse gets tired of asking for forgiveness and the offended spouse gets tired of raising the issue. So the behavior continues, and grudges grow. Steady communication keeps the issue on the surface, where it can be dealt with.

Another problem is that the apology-and-forgiveness process can be watered down. When the problem is chronic, the words "I'm sorry" and "I forgive you" are repeated so often that they can be misunderstood.

"I'm sorry" can begin to mean "I'm sorry that you're upset about this (but hey, that's just the way I am)."

It *should* mean "I was wrong; I'll do everything possible not to do it again."

"I forgive you" can be understood as "It's all right; no problem; no damage done."

It *should* mean "Yes, you hurt me, but I will not let that action poison our relationship."

Whether the offense is as major as an extramarital affair or as minor as leaving the cap off the toothpaste, the full process of forgiveness requires repentance rather than excuses.

THE UNREPENTANT PARTNER

What if your spouse never asks for forgiveness?

There are reasons that he or she may not ask for forgiveness. The most obvious is that your spouse doesn't think he or she did anything wrong. You can debate the facts of the case forever, but at some point you may need to make a unilateral decision to forgive. Just let it go. You let go of it even though your partner doesn't admit there was an offense.

Let's reexamine the incident between Wilma and Fred but change it just slightly. Let's say that Wilma knows that she checked every box and that she did not throw away Fred's memorabilia. She suspects that Fred threw it away carelessly years ago, but that he just wants someone else to blame.

Fred believes wholeheartedly that Wilma threw away his stuff and that now she's just lying about it. Neither one can apologize—both genuinely believe they're innocent. In a case like this, if there is an apology, it's probably an appeasement: "If I did something wrong, I'm sorry." You're just saying the debate is not worth wrecking the relationship. That's a noble decision sometimes, but if you find these impasses are happening regularly, it can become frustrating, even maddening. (And watch out for the passive-aggressive response, offering a quick apology but determining to get even later.)

The solution approach is helpful in a case like this. Rather than focusing on the past problem, look toward the future. Where do you want to go from here? From this perspective, it doesn't matter who's right and who's wrong. What will it take to live together peacefully? You can agree to disagree about the facts of the case—just agree to move on.

The two partners can employ the act-as-if method. They give each other the benefit of the doubt. Fred may still believe that Wilma threw away his stuff, but to keep peace he decides to act as if she didn't. He releases his grudge, even though

Wilma never agrees to having done wrong.

There's another reason a person might refuse to ask for forgiveness: He or she may be lying.

Let's return to the case of Art and Sylvia, but change the facts again. Let's say that Sylvia knows that Art is having an affair, but when she confronts him about it, he angrily denies all wrongdoing. He might even accuse her of being paranoid or crazy. But the facts are clear—Sylvia has undeniable evidence that Art is having an affair, even though he's not willing to take responsibility for it. In such a situation, how should Sylvia proceed with her forgiveness?

In Matthew 18:15-17, Jesus spoke about trying to make things right with someone who has wronged you. If the initial confrontation with the person doesn't result in repentance and reconciliation, Jesus said, "Take one or two others along." This makes a lot of sense, even in a marital situation. You need perspective. With just the two of you, you could argue forever, your word against your spouse's. But if you bring a counselor into the picture, or a church leader, or some mutually trusted friends, you can better establish the facts of the situation.

In counseling, we sometimes set up an *intervention*, where we call together significant friends and relatives to confront a person about a problem he or she has been denying. This is especially helpful if the person is dealing with some kind of addiction. In such cases, a certified addiction counselor would be the best one to lead the intervention. In cases of chronic affairs or lying, mature Christian friends or church leaders might be best.[1]

Why do you need to get someone else in on your personal problems? Well, maybe you *are* being paranoid. If so, the third party can tell you so. If you have undeniable evidence, then the third party can confirm it, and your spouse will be forced to own up to his or her wrongdoing.

The purpose is not one-upmanship or humiliation, but agreement. If your relationship is going to be healthy again, you and your spouse need to agree on where you both stand. Often just the threat of airing your dirty laundry before others will force the errant spouse to admit the transgression.

What if your spouse refuses to see a counselor or some other third party? There may be legitimate concerns about who the third party is; if so, negotiate this as best you can. But if your spouse stubbornly refuses to see anyone, you should see a counselor or church leader on your own. This will give you much-needed support and valuable advice on how to proceed.

What if your spouse sees the third party with you, but continues to claim innocence? Jesus said that if the errant person will not listen to the two or three witnesses, "tell it to the church" (Matthew 18:17). In their efforts to follow this teaching, some churches have public denouncements or messages in the church bulletin, but we should remember the goal of this whole process: *love* and *restoration*. I believe the church can and should have a part in healing the marriages of its members. This can be done in a number of gentle ways, though there may be a point where an unrepentant philanderer may need to be reprimanded by the church or even removed from its membership. (The church should also provide special support for the wronged spouse.)

> *We often take the easy way out, and avoid the hard work that's needed for forgiveness to take place.*

If the offending person refuses to listen to the church's reprimand, Jesus said he should be treated as a nonbeliever. This does not mean that the person is no longer a Christian, but it does mean that we can no longer expect godly behavior from this person. We should still treat the person with the love and respect we would show to any unbeliever, but our relationship with this person changes. What's more, this person's *marriage* changes.

Let's say Art continues to deny the affair he had. Sylvia and Art meet with their pastor and a few trusted church leaders, who look at the evidence and support Sylvia's charges. They urge Art to repent, but he refuses. After all of this, according to Jesus' teaching, Sylvia needs to treat Art as an unbeliever. This does not mean she has to divorce him, but there will be a new distance in the relationship. She needs to establish firm boundaries, protecting herself from further hurt from Art.

Can she still forgive Art? Yes, though it's not easy. Her

response is like the cry from the cross: "Father, forgive them, for they do not know what they are doing" (Luke 23:34). Sylvia can decide on her own to drop the issue — not to excuse it or shift the blame, but simply to say, "I will not let this pain and hate rule my life anymore."

We have seen interventions work with many couples. We have seen them work for alcoholic marriages, for abusive and adulterous relationships, for spending and gambling problems, for husbands who refuse to work, and for wives who refuse to care for their children. Sometimes people do admit their wrongdoing and seek restoration. In those cases, forgiveness is easier. It's never a cinch, but it's easier when the person is seeking forgiveness.

The worst case of all is when a wrong is done and never acknowledged by either party. One suffers in pain, the other in guilt, but both suffer in silence. The bonds of matrimony soon fray as forgiveness is neither sought nor offered. That's why we encourage solution-based approaches to mend the marriage relationship.

Forgiveness can set a person free. It can breathe new life into a tired marriage. But it's hard work. Forgiveness is not a shrug of the shoulders — "Hey, no problem." Yes, there *is* a problem! The forgiving person often has to be willing to wake the partner up, to figuratively "shake the offender by the shoulders" and say, "Hey, look! You hurt me. I am willing to let that go, but we've got to do something to fix this relationship. I want you to work with me. I need your help."

SOLUTION WORKSHOP TEN

GOAL: Map out the road of forgiveness.

1. When my spouse is upset with me what am I most likely to notice? (Pick no more than three—continued on next page.)

HE		SHE
☐	Glaring Eyes	☐
☐	The Silent Treatment	☐
☐	A Slow Burn	☐

HE		SHE
☐	A Nuclear Explosion	☐
☐	A Cold Shoulder	☐
☐	Heightened Emotions	☐
☐	Apathy	☐

2. Once the issue is discussed and considered forgiven, which spouse do you think has a harder time letting go of the hurt?

3. What signs might you notice that would indicate that things are still bothering your spouse?

HE		SHE
☐	Glaring Eyes	☐
☐	The Silent Treatment	☐
☐	A Slow Burn	☐
☐	A Nuclear Explosion	☐
☐	A Cold Shoulder	☐
☐	Heightened Emotions	☐
☐	Apathy	☐

For the Wife

4. Is there something for which you need to ask for forgiveness from your husband? What?

5. Is there something you need to forgive your husband for? What?

For the Husband

4. Is there something for which you need to ask for forgiveness from your wife? What?

5. Is there something you need to forgive your wife for? What?

For Both

6. Is there any restitution that needs to be made? What?

7. How can you show you are truly repentant?

8. How can you show your spouse that complete forgiveness has taken place?

Next time a hurt occurs in your marriage, practice the act-as-if technique. Act as if you have completely forgiven your spouse, even though it still might be bothering you. There are many times you will find that your feelings will follow your behaviors.

If you hit an impasse, try the miracle question. Imagine that after you go to bed tonight, while you are sleeping, God does a miracle and completely heals you of all your resentment and bad feelings toward your spouse, and He heals your spouse of all resentment and bad feelings toward you. When you wake up in the morning how would you know that the miracle had happened?

9. What would be different?

10. How would you behave toward your spouse?

11. How would your spouse treat you?

Now begin acting in those ways toward each other and see what happens.

▼ ▼

Changing Your Marriage By Changing Yourself

Susan is in the process of detaching from her husband. She is not divorcing him, just detaching for the sake of her own growth and sanity. She and Craig got married for all the right reasons. Both Christians, they had known each other since high school. When they got together, friends and family were thrilled. No one saw the potential problems in their marriage.

After the wedding, things were fine for a while. But after a couple of financial disasters, Craig began to change. They lost their home, their savings, and then Craig was out of work. In addition, the losses took their toll on Craig's self-image, contributing to his ongoing depression.

At first Susan assumed he was just going through a bad time and that he would get over it soon. But week after week, month after month, the problems persisted. After much prodding, Craig agreed to see a counselor, but counseling was cut short when Craig announced that the counselor was an idiot, an utter waste of his time and money.

Susan wondered what had happened to the sweet man she'd married. Craig's whole temperament had soured. As miserable as could be, he tended to make life miserable for Susan as well. Susan tried to be helpful and uplifting, but that didn't work. She tried talking to Craig, but he didn't want to talk. She tried to get him out with other people, but he wanted to be left alone. Then she tried to get someone from the church to come and talk with him, but that made him angry. Susan felt that she could do nothing right. Each thing she tried only made Craig's attitude worse. She felt Craig drifting away from her, and she didn't know how to stop it or even slow it down. What could she do to change him?

Susan decided to try one more thing—she sought counseling for herself.

"I want to save my marriage," she said. "But my husband shows no desire to change. What can I do?"

It's a tough question. Many therapists would conclude that there's nothing Susan can do by herself to save the marriage, saying, "It takes two to tango." But the solution-based approach *can* be applied by just one person in the marriage, with significant results.

Ideally, of course, every marriage involves two people who are willing and motivated to work together at improving their relationship. But occasionally one partner will shut down, showing no interest in working through marital problems. This makes it more difficult to make positive changes, but not impossible.

The key to these changes will not be manipulation or pressure tactics used against your reluctant spouse, but how effectively you can change yourself.

In family systems theory, there is a strong belief in the idea that a change in one member of the family automatically changes the whole family system. Picture a mobile, perhaps something you made as a kid by stringing various objects from a coat hanger. Hit just one of the hanging items and what happens? *All* the objects dance and sway. A family is like that, with each member affected by a change that happens to any other. So if you want your marriage to change, you first must change yourself.

The Bible indicates this same principle in 1 Peter 3:1-2 (NASB), instructing the wives of "disobedient" husbands to win them "without a word by [your] godly behavior . . . as they observe your chaste and respectful behavior." When you change your behavior, even slightly, it can create ripple effects that can completely change your marriage. In Susan's case, I* would have

---

*All first person pronouns in this chapter refer to Tom Whiteman.

preferred to have both Susan and Craig in my office, but I'll take what I can get. So will Susan. Her marriage will not change as much or as fast as it would with both partners working on it, but it will change.

Don't get me wrong. I'm not implying that it's somehow Susan's fault that the marriage is stagnated. She may not be doing anything *wrong,* but she could do something *different,* which might elicit a different response from Craig. Remember one of our basic rules of solution-based therapy: *If what you're doing isn't working, try something else.*

If you want your marriage to change, you first must change yourself.

Taking a solution approach with Susan, I focused on three principles. *First,* I asked her what she had been doing to work on the marriage. She described her efforts to help her husband, encourage her husband, and to get him out of his rut. Obviously this wasn't working. I urged Susan to take a different approach, acknowledge her husband's disappointments and feelings of failure, and then back away.

She rehearsed this in my office—telling him in a respectful way that he had good reason to be sad and discouraged, empathizing with his pain. But then, I said, she should go out with friends and have a good time. She could invite Craig to come along, but she knew he never wanted to go out. If he complained about her going out without him, I suggested, she should just say, "I really need to get out, but I understand if you're not up to it. You have a lot on your mind. Why don't you stay home and relax while I go out?"

Second, I invited Susan to consider the *quicksand theory.* Some relationships are like quicksand: the more you struggle, the more you go under. The solution is to stop struggling and to let yourself float. In Susan's case, I thought she was struggling too hard. She needed to relax a bit and let Craig motivate himself to do his own work.

Third, I asked Susan, "What would make you feel better?" She proceeded to tell me how she wished Craig would change and be happy once again.

"You just told me how you want Craig to feel," I replied. "What do *you* need? What would make *you* feel better?"

This time Susan thought about it awhile. "I'd like to enjoy my life again. I want to laugh and have fun. I want to have a close relationship and know that I'm loved."

"These are all good things — and certainly normal desires," I explained. "Since you can't force Craig to fulfill your desires, are there legitimate ways for you to meet these needs and still honor your marriage?"

Susan told of good times she had enjoyed with her best friend Lisa, dining together, talking about old times, and laughing until their sides hurt. She could always count on Lisa to lift her spirits. Certainly this friend could never take the place of a loving husband, but she could use that friendship to meet some of the needs Craig was neglecting. There were other appropriate friendships, too, that might provide her with much-needed affirmation and emotional support.

All three principles pointed to the same recommendation. Susan needed to detach from Craig, finding legitimate fulfillment in her friendships and other activities. This was not a marital separation but an emotional distancing. They would still live together, and she would continue to respect him, but she would no longer cling to him, begging him to meet all her needs. When he was ready to reinvest himself in the marriage (*if* that would ever happen), she would be there. But she was going to stop beating her head against this brick wall. She could live her own life.

And the result? Susan stopped trying to talk Craig out of his foul moods. Even when he would go on drinking binges, she would not nag him about it. She empathized with his "dreadful" life, but did not harp on it. Instead, she went shopping, helped in the women's ministry at church, and visited with her friend Lisa.

This surprised Craig at first. "What do you mean you're going out? What am I supposed to do?"

"You must have had a difficult day, dear. Why don't you just stay home and rest?" Susan answered. "Maybe next time you could come along. We could invite Lisa's husband too and all go out to dinner."

"He's boring," Craig mumbled.

"That's okay," said Susan. "You don't have to come along." With that, she left for the evening.

After a few weeks and several of those nights out, Craig began to see that Susan was serious about her new ways of coping. He stopped getting attention for his negativity, so he started to say he was feeling a little better. In fact, he was feeling so good, maybe they could go out the next weekend.

Your changes may throw your system into turmoil for a while, but eventually it will turn out for the best.

The system was starting to change.

Susan still struggled with a husband who dragged his feet and tended to complain, but whenever he did, she paid little attention to him and went on with her life. Craig began to see that, if he wanted attention, the best way to get it was to interact with others and to be pleasant. His drinking subsided, and they began to go out regularly as a couple. Susan was encouraged by the change and felt much better about her life. She no longer lived to make Craig happy. She had learned how to take care of herself.

UNHAPPY ENDINGS?

What if Craig hadn't changed? What if Susan's new strategy resulted in no difference or even worse moods and increased drinking? Well, Susan could try some other method. If at first you don't succeed. . . .

Whether or not these methods succeeded, Susan learned an important lesson. Ultimately she is responsible only for herself. She cannot change her husband, and she cannot be responsible for the changes he needs to make. She can change herself, however, and that is her only route to a better marriage.

I have counseled other wives who came, all alone, to seek help for their marriages (and a few such husbands, but not many). As with Susan, I urge these women to make changes in themselves, take responsibility for their own lives, and release their responsibility for their recalcitrant partners. This often results in improved self-esteem and better lives for these people. But I must admit that these changes sometimes worsen the marriage.

Sometimes an abused wife will learn to speak up for herself, yet the change might lead to more abuse. Finally, for her own safety, she has to leave her home. Or, after turning a blind eye for years, a wife might finally confront her husband about his infidelity, only to find that he files for divorce.

Changing yourself for the better will not bring you and your spouse closer together. But don't let that keep you from making the healthy changes you need to make. Your changes will rock the mobile a little, maybe a lot. You may throw your system into turmoil for a while, but eventually the right steps can change things for the best.

If your spouse *does* decide to work on the relationship, then you will be in a healthier place, better able to know what you want and how to interact in better ways. But if your spouse never changes or decides to leave you, then you are also better off because you have sought to honor God with your life, and that makes your life fulfilling and complete. Marriages that cloak abuse or infidelity do not honor God.

SURVIVING ON YOUR OWN

What is *detachment?*

Detachment does not necessarily mean divorce, just distance. It is often emotional, sometimes physical or sexual, and in extreme cases geographical (you move out). Whatever form it takes, you create a different balance and new boundaries in the marriage—walls that protect you from hurt or abuse.

This is easier said than done. Your partner may blame you for ruining the relationship, but you are actually ruining the unhealthy patterns that have governed your relationship. You are trying to restore the relationship on better terms.

Detachment must be done with love. As you pull away from dependence on your spouse, avoid the temptation to pay back or get even. It's a tough love that creates distance between a husband and a wife. In *Love Must Be Tough*, James Dobson says it's an issue of *respect*. Speaking of wives whose husbands have affairs, he says, "They share the same basic problem. Their husbands feel trapped in suffocating relationships with women they clearly disrespect."

In dating relationships, Dobson says, you don't coerce someone into loving you. It doesn't work that way. "If begging and pleading are ineffective methods of attracting a member of the opposite sex during the dating days, why do victims of bad marriages use the same groveling techniques to hold a drifting spouse? They are only increasing the depth of disrespect by the one who is escaping."

If you're in a destructive relationship, then for your own protection you need to build some fences.

Dobson recommends that the wronged spouse "open the cage door," setting the other spouse free to leave the relationship if that's what he or she wants.

"Look at it this way. Verbal bludgeoning never made anyone more loving or sensitive. You simply can't tear your spouse to pieces and then expect him or her to meet your emotional needs. People aren't made that way. Rather than attacking and driving away your unresponsive spouse, draw your partner in your direction by taking the pressure off, by pulling backward a bit, by avoiding the worn out accusations and complaints, by appearing to need him less, by *actually* needing him less. As you become more of a person in your own right, you will be more fun to be with. Happiness (and self-fulfillment) is a marvelous magnet to the human personality."[1]

How can you accomplish this? By creating boundaries in the relationship, boundaries that help you to distinguish yourself from your spouse. As most teenagers have said to their parents, "Get a life!" You need a life of your own to fall back on while you continue to try to build a life with your spouse.

"Good fences make good neighbors," wrote Robert Frost in his poem "Mending Wall." He was onto something.

I had a neighbor who was aggravated by my leaves blowing in his yard. He liked to remove the autumn leaves weekly, while

I preferred to let them all fall and rake them just once. Of course my leaves frequently decorated his yard, and this created some tension. We became much better neighbors once we put up a fence, one that would catch my leaves before they blew into his yard.

In most marriages, we seek that *one flesh* relationship—no secrets, no walls, no boundaries. Bonding occurs over time and fences disappear one by one as the partners feel safe with each other.

But there are times when we *need* fences to provide safety in the relationship. Marriages that are not working often have one person who is doing all the work, while the other does little or nothing—just as I was unwilling to rake the leaves. Putting up the fence kept one neighbor (me) from taking advantage of the other. One-sided marriages need fences too, to protect one partner from taking advantage of the other.

Ideally, these fences wouldn't be necessary. But if you're in a destructive relationship, you need to build some fences for your own protection. You need to find some workable solutions for your daily frustrations and conflicts. Without your partner's cooperation, you cannot fix all the underlying problems, but you *can* find ways to get through the day. Find ways to continue growing on your own. One of the hallmarks of solution-based therapy is its focus on what *can* be done to improve things rather than on what *should* be done but never will. The following suggestions will not only help protect you in a bad situation, but they will also help you to succeed on your own, should that be necessary.

TAKE AWAY YOUR PARTNER'S ABILITY TO RUIN YOUR DAY

One sure sign that you're overly attached is when your spouse can say or do something that ruins your day, your week, or even a longer period of time. We all have emotional hot buttons, things our spouses know will really get to us. Consciously or unconsciously, spouses learn to use these when they want to get back at us for something or when they want to manipulate us.

Think of these as emotional strings. Your spouse pulls a string here or there and finds that you blow up, make a fool of yourself, or walk away and sulk for days. You are manipulated like a puppet. The only way to change the situation is to cut the strings. Know where your own emotional strings are and decide in advance not to be manipulated. See the manipulation as it begins to happen and steel yourself against those attacks.

REDUCE EXPECTATIONS

Early in this book we discussed unrealistic expectations for your marriage. But if you're stuck in a very unfulfilling marriage, you may need to let go of *all* your expectations. I know one golf widow who has found the only way for her to survive is by expecting that her husband will never spend his day off at home. It may not be fair or right, but by expecting nothing, she no longer gets as angry when he goes golfing—and occasionally she is pleasantly surprised when he stays home on a Saturday (only when it rains).

Isn't this just giving up on your marriage? No. You still hold the hope that things may turn around for you someday, but you know that no amount of pushing will get you where you want to be. If you maintain high expectations, you will continue to be disappointed. Just downgrade those expectations to the level of patient hopes. This will limit your disappointment and may yield some surprises.

RELEASE ALL ATTEMPTS AT CONTROLLING YOUR SPOUSE

You may be trying to reform an alcoholic, bring a sinner to repentance, or just trying to get your spouse to appreciate you more. No matter how noble the cause, trying to control your spouse will only frustrate you both. Even if you fear your partner will fall apart without your control, you need to give up that control.

Cutting the strings of dependency and control goes both ways. As you cut the emotional strings by which your spouse controls you, you also need to cut the controls you have on your spouse. As long as you control your partner's behavior, your partner doesn't have to take personal responsibility. Both of you will be better off if you stop trying to control or change.

If you're a control freak, this won't be easy. Monitor your

controlling behavior and then curtail it. There are a million little ways—words, looks, actions, gestures—by which we exert control. Hunt for these and try to stop. If you think it wise, announce your intention to give up your controlling behavior and ask your spouse to point out *when* you seem to be controlling. But the main shift here is philosophical: You're deciding that you do not have the right to dictate (or manipulate) what your spouse does.

FIND NEW SOURCES OF SECURITY

In a bad marriage, your sense of safety is threatened. The partner you thought you could count on has fallen short of your expectations. You have been betrayed, abused, ignored. If your marriage was your only safe haven in a stormy world, then your plight is bad indeed. To whom can you turn?

Even if you're sure you are changing your spouse for the better, you need to let go of efforts to control or manipulate.

I have seen several cases where domineering husbands take control of their wives by discouraging or forbidding their relationships with old friends or family members. It is a very effective ploy, cutting their wives off from any outside sources of security. In some cases, the husbands pull their wives away from church involvements, depriving them of their spiritual support.

If your marriage has proven unsafe, you need to restore old friendships or make new ones. Find the security you need in people other than your spouse. Of course I am not suggesting that you seek romantic love or sexual involvement with others. Be especially careful in friendships with those of the opposite sex—you are vulnerable to temptation right now. It may be best to develop your strongest friendships within your own gender.

And look to God for His strength in these trying times. I have known many who, in the pit of despair over their marriage, have cried out to the Lord and found a closer, more fulfilling relationship with Him. The Lord offers to come alongside us and comfort us when we need Him.

FIND NEW SOURCES OF SIGNIFICANCE

People find great significance in a good marriage. I regularly talk with people who are proud of being good wives and mothers, good husbands and fathers. They know they have an important role in their homes, and they feel good about it.

But this can become a problem when your spouse is your *only* source of significance, when you say, "I am somebody because my spouse loves me," or, "I would be nothing without my mate." That may sound very romantic, and you can get away with it if the relationship is healthy and balanced.

The best way to increase your sense of value is to find out what you do well, and then do it!

But we're talking about unfulfilling relationships, bad marriages, embattled homes. It's a sad fact that some marriages do more to destroy a person's sense of significance than to build it. As you try to detach and set new boundaries, you need to find new supports for your self-respect. Part of boundary setting is learning to find security and significance in your relationship with God and within yourself.

One of the best ways to increase your sense of value is to find out what you do well, and then do it! A marriage can be an incubator of your personal abilities, helping them develop and mature, or it can be a closet, hiding them (even from yourself). If your talents have been hidden away, you need to take them out, dust them off, and use them.

Let's say you enjoy gourmet cooking, but your spouse always finds fault with the food you prepare. Then find others who will be able to appreciate your skills. Invite friends over every month for a gourmet meal. Cook for the church dinner. Find a ministry for hungry people and offer your culinary services. You might even open your own business.

Don't bury your talents in the ground anymore. Discover what God has empowered you to do, and do it!

But don't just find value in your *accomplishments*; let your *relationships* enhance your sense of significance, too. Be a support to your new friends and listen to their words of encouragement. After years of hearing nothing but criticism, it may be difficult to hear compliments—but you need them. Find friends who will build you up.[2]

BECOME MORE SELF-SUFFICIENT

You probably know widows who were totally helpless when their husbands died. The husbands wrote the checks, made the buying decisions, even drove the car, and their wives relied on them. But when the husbands die, their widows don't know how to do anything.

The same thing often happens with divorce or abandonment. Wives who were overly dependent on their husbands have to get a crash course in reality.

Detachment *may* mean that you take more responsibility for the details of your life. If you're married to a gambler or a spendaholic, it's a good idea to get separate checking accounts and credit cards. But if your spouse seeks to control you by controlling your money that may also be a reason for separate finances.

You may need to get a job or take classes to improve your job skills. Don't expect support from your spouse. He or she may resent your growing independence and try to thwart it. But press on. Remember that you are trying to improve the marriage by changing the destructive patterns, and that means changing yourself. A stronger you can mean a stronger marriage.

If your marriage is in pretty good shape, these measures are not necessary. But remember that we're talking about relationships that are somewhat toxic. Things have to change. Perhaps these self-strengthening moves will heal the marriage. If they don't, then at least you are more prepared for the consequences.

▼ ▼ ▼

"It Takes One to Tango." That's a chapter title in Michele Weiner-Davis's book *Divorce-Busting,* and we love it. Except it's not really true. In order for your marriage to be completely restored, both husband and wife need to work at it. But it takes one to *start* the tango. It takes one to invite the other to dance. It takes one to say, "Hey, pal, the music's playing and we've just been sitting here for the last five years. Let's boogie!"

Maybe your spouse won't dance with you. Allow for that possibility. You can't force your partner to join you. But *you* hear the music, and you're spinning and sliding and gliding. Your partner's a fool not to take your hand and get in on the action, but at least you're having fun.

SOLUTION WORKSHOP ELEVEN

GOAL: Find ways to move forward despite a spouse who stays put.

1. What needs do you have? Examine the list of needs and then add a few of your own that we may have missed. When you think about the people who meet your needs, recognize that we all need more than a spouse to meet our needs. Don't be afraid to write "no one" if you find that those needs are being neglected.

MY NEEDS AND WHO MEETS THEM

Accountability
Best friend
Conversational needs
Counseling concerns
Emotional encouragement
Fellowship
Financial needs
Mentor
Safety
Security
Self-worth
Sexual needs
Significance
Social needs
Spiritual guidance
Others (name them)

2. As you look back at needs that are not being met or ones that are only partially being met, begin to think about people or things in your life that might help to meet those needs. Try the

exercise again, but this time list others whose assistance you might enlist to fulfill unmet needs.

My Needs and Who Might Meet Them

Accountability
Best friend
Conversational needs
Counseling concerns
Emotional encouragement
Fellowship
Financial needs
Mentor
Safety
Security
Self-worth
Sexual needs
Significance
Social needs
Spiritual guidance
Others (name them)

3. What steps can you take this week, this month, and this year to get your needs met? What needs should you put on hold for a while?

4. a. For example, perhaps you said you need to take care of your financial security by getting a better job. What steps do you need to take?

   ▼ Go back to school?
   ▼ Update your resume?
   ▼ Begin to interview?
   ▼ Others (name them)

   b. Select up to three unmet needs and in the space below come up with three possible ways you could work toward meeting each of those needs.

▼ ▼

The Road Ahead:
A Conclusion

M arriage is great. Marriage is difficult.
Fishermen know that the best trout swim in rapid streams. The ones that spend most of their lives in gentle surroundings don't grow very much, but those that have to fight their way upstream against powerful currents—these develop in size and strength.

The same is true of marriage. A couple of newlyweds may think their love is strong; they are so totally wrapped up in each other. "Marriage is great," they say. "Ain't love grand?" Yet they hardly know what love is.

When they move from infatuation to negotiation, they may think something is terribly wrong—but they've just been thrown in the river. "Marriage is difficult," they cry. "Love hurts." But their love will grow as they swim against the current, as they fight their own laziness, selfishness, dependence, and independence to develop a solid relationship, and ultimately a mature love.

Marriage is great. Marriage is difficult.

Now that you have read this book, you are automatically empowered to make your marriage all it can be. No more petty fights. No more icy glares. You will now express yourself thoroughly and listen perfectly. Right?

Guess again.

Your marriage will always have conflict. Put two human beings in the same vicinity for fifty years, and there will be a few disagreements. (A few?) But conflict means that you care—about yourself, about your spouse, about life in general. Conflict means your relationship is alive—and kicking. This book is not about putting an end to conflict, but I hope it can help you *use* conflict as a positive process of change.

Jesus told His followers, "In this world you will have trouble" (John 16:33). You could say the same thing about marriage. Jesus was clear that the Christian life is no Sunday stroll in the garden, but rather it is an experience that is challenging, and hard, and very, very good. Paul gives encouragement: "We also rejoice in our sufferings, because we know that suffering produces perseverance; perseverance, character; and character, hope" (Romans 5:3-4).

Similarly our marriages develop sound character and hope as we work through our conflicts. Not even Christian marriages are immune from troubles. Oh, you will have a few Sunday strolls when all is right with your relationship, but you will also have arguments, cold shoulders, manipulation, and ambushes. Don't let it shake your faith when these things happen. It does not mean you're a bad Christian; it does not mean your spouse is a bad Christian—it just means you're human. In bumper sticker language, "Christians aren't perfect, just forgiven." And forgiving each other can be a tricky business.

GETTING THERE FROM HERE

Paul and Karen got married right out of college. Both committed Christians, they were sure their marriage would last forever because they were determined to keep God at the center of their relationship. But time and familiarity took a toll on their love. It was at a Fresh Start divorce recovery seminar that I* first met Karen, depressed and broken. She was separated from Paul and didn't know if she could ever go back.

Karen blamed Paul for the distance in their relationship.

*All first person pronouns in this chapter refer to Tom Whiteman.

Even in their first year of marriage, he was playing softball two nights a week and working two other nights. That evolved into working late every night and business trips twice a month. When Karen confronted Paul about his schedule, he quoted the Bible to her—she needed to submit to him and support his work. This hard work, he said, was a sacrifice he made for the good of the marriage. This made her feel guilty for being so demanding.

Then, without even discussing it with her, Paul accepted a promotion at work, which meant more travel. That was the last straw. If he wanted distance, he could have all the distance he wanted!

"I'm still young and still have a chance at a fulfilling relationship," Karen told me later, in a counseling session. "I don't want to wait around until I'm old and gray for him to come home. These are supposed to be the best years of my life, but instead I'm lonely and depressed."

I asked if I could talk to Paul about their situation. Karen was hesitant to let me get in touch with him but finally conceded.

To my surprise, Paul was anxious to meet with me and expressed a strong desire to do whatever it would take to get his wife back. "We're both Christians," he kept saying. "She can't leave me like this." While I could empathize with his pain, I also knew that many Christians had split up for similar reasons. Still, I commended him for his desire to work through the present crisis.

Individually, and then together, Karen and Paul met with me. At first, Karen refused to move back in with him. He was promising to change, but she didn't trust him.

I asked them the miracle question: "If you were to go to sleep and a miracle happened, so that all your problems were solved, what would your life be like? How would things be different?"

Their answers gave me some hope. Karen was part of Paul's ideal picture, and Paul was in Karen's ideal life, but in both of their descriptions, Paul was no longer working at his present job. I suggested that maybe the job was the problem and that they should both blame the job rather than each other.

Eventually we got around to negotiations. What would it take for these two to get back together? Paul still had to work for a living but could he change his goals to leave more room for Karen?

They agreed to date each other for a few months, while continuing to live apart. Karen would observe Paul's changes and see whether his words would be backed up by his actions.

Paul did change, and Karen learned to trust him again. They moved back in together and recommitted themselves to their marriage—but there were still conditions. Paul was to work late only one night a week and take only one trip a month. Trips were to be no more than three nights away, and he promised to be home by 6:00 P.M. all other nights.

Today they are doing well together. Karen is expecting their first child, and Paul is sticking to his promises. (These will be even more important now that he's going to be a dad.)

When I think of Karen and Paul, I think of another Paul, the apostle, and how he characterized his life: "Forgetting what is behind and straining toward what is ahead, I press on toward the goal" (Philippians 3:13-14). He wasn't speaking of marriage in particular, but he could have been. A good marriage requires that we forget bad patterns of the past and that we press on toward the goal.

KEEP MOVING

People get used to bad marriages. They find a certain security in the fact that he will watch TV in the living room so she'll be asleep before he comes to bed, or that she really doesn't respect what he does for a living, or that they mustn't ever talk about certain subjects. They're just too tired to fight anymore, so they just walk around each other, avoiding any real engagement. Oh, there might be an explosion here and there, but generally there's an uneasy truce, a stalemate. They pursue their separate careers and bounce the kids back and forth. They stay together for the kids' sake, or for financial reasons, or because they just don't know where else to go.

Friends at church have no clue—they're a fine, upstanding couple in the community. But inside their hearts is the nagging sense that this is not what they signed up for. Their relationship should be better, much better. If only she would. . . . If only he would. . . .

People get stuck. Maybe that's where you are. You progressed from the infatuation stage to the energetic conflict stage and descended into the boredom stage. "Mature love" is something that Christian authors write books about, but it seems out of reach, doesn't it?

We hope this book gets you unstuck. There are no magical cures, no surefire techniques, just ideas that will get you talking together about how to break the impasse, how to move forward, how to grow again. Even solution-based therapy won't do anything by itself—unless you make it happen. But it's not rocket science, it's common sense stuff: Listen, talk, dream, share. You can do it.

If both of you are committed to the relationship, then you need to agree together that it needs to be done, that you have to get back on the road again. You may have grown used to your bad patterns. Growing a marriage takes time, effort, and patience. It's easier to watch a ball game or go out with friends. Marriage is more difficult. But marriage can also be great. You'll see.

▼ ▼

Notes

Looking to the Future, Not the Past: An Introduction

1. Elizabeth Gleick, "Should This Marriage Be Saved?" *Time,* 27 February 1995, pp. 48-56.
2. John Gottman, *Why Marriages Succeed or Fail: And How You Can Make Yours Last* (New York: Simon & Shuster, 1994), p. 128.

Chapter One: Unmasking Marital Myths

1. Michele Weiner-Davis, *Divorce Busting* (New York: Simon & Shuster, 1992), p. 41.
2. Thomas Bartlett, "Marital Disruption and Christian Orthodoxy: Reaction and Adjustment to Divorce" (Ann Arbor, Mich.: University Microfilms, 1989).
3. Weiner-Davis, p. 58.
4. Weiner-Davis, p. 62.

Chapter Two: Stages of Marriage: Where Are You?

1. The stages are adapted from Harville Hendrix, *Getting the Love You Want* (New York: Henry Holt & Co., 1988), chapters 4–5.
2. Hendrix, pp. 42-43.
3. Hendrix, p. 45.
4. Donald Lathrop, comment in response to Howard Halpern's

article "Falling in Love Is Not Enough," *Journal of Couples Therapy* 2, no. 3 (1991): p. 23.

5. Alexander Jasnow, "And Then There Were Two," *Journal of Couples Therapy* 2, no. 3 (1991): p. 52.

6. Petruska Clarkson, "Facets of the Dance," *Journal of Couples Therapy* 2, no. 3 (1991): p. 74.

7. Quoted by Beth Azar, "Respectful Negotiation Is the Key to Marital Bliss," *APA Monitor*, September 1995, p. 10.

8. Patricia O'Hanlon Hudson and William Hudson O'Hanlon, *Rewriting Love Stories* (New York: Norton, 1991), p. 76.

9. M. Scott Peck, "Further Along the Road Less Traveled," (New York: Simon & Shuster, 1987), audiotape.

10. Frank Pitman, *Private Lies* (New York: Norton, 1989), p. 92.

CHAPTER FOUR: MAKING YOUR MARRIAGE A PLACE OF SAFETY

1. Larry Hof, "Treating Couples—Managing Conflict: The Creative Use of Differences" (seminar of the Marriage Council of Philadelphia, 15 November 1991), Session 1, "The Nature of Conflict."

2. Jerome A. Travers, "Love and Marriage and Other Silly Delusions," *Journal of Couples Therapy* 2, no. 3 (1991): p. 85.

3. Harville Hendrix, *Getting the Love You Want* (New York: Henry Holt & Co., 1988), p. 69.

CHAPTER FIVE: IDENTIFYING YOUR COMMUNICATION STYLES

1. Sharon Begley, "Gray Matter: The New Science of the Brain," *Newsweek*, 27 March 1995, pp. 48-54.

2. Begley, pp. 48-54.

3. John Gray, *Men Are from Mars, Women Are from Venus* (New York: Harper Collins, 1992). Gray's book is helpful on this entire subject of gender differences. Of the plethora of books available, we also recommend Deborah Tannen, *You Just Don't Understand* (New York: Simon & Shuster, 1991); Thomas Whiteman and Randy Petersen, *Men Who Love Too Little* (Nashville: Nelson, 1994); Robert Hicks, *The Masculine Journey* (Colorado Springs: NavPress, 1994); Robert and Cynthia Hicks, *The Feminine Journey* (Colorado Springs: NavPress, 1995).

CHAPTER SIX: CREATIVE COMMUNICATION

1. Deborah Tannen, *You Just Don't Understand* (New York: Simon & Schuster, 1991), pp. 26-28. See also Tannen's *That's Not What I Meant: How Conversational Style Makes or Breaks Your Relations with Others* (New York: Morrow, 1986).
2. John Gray, *Men Are from Mars, Women Are from Venus* (New York: Harper Collins, 1992), p. 88.
3. Gray, pp. 84-85.
4. Catherine Johnson, "Talk Your Way to a Long-Lasting Love," *New Woman*, June 1993, p. 48.
5. Adapted from Harville Hendrix, *Getting the Love You Want* (New York: Henry Holt & Co., 1988), pp. 216-17; and Howard Markman, Scott Stanley, and Susan Blumberg, "The Prep Approach," *Fighting for Your Marriage* audiotape series (Denver, Colo.: PREP, Inc., 1994).
6. Maryhelen Snyder, "The Co-Construction of New Meanings in Couple Relationships: A Psychoeducational Model That Promotes Mutual Empowerment," *Journal of Couples Therapy* 2, no. 4 (1991): p. 48.

CHAPTER SEVEN: WHAT DOESN'T WORK: DESTRUCTIVE PATTERNS IN CONFLICT RESOLUTION

1. Adapted from Michele Weiner-Davis, *Divorce Busting* (New York: Simon & Shuster, 1992), pp. 128-158.

CHAPTER EIGHT: WHAT DOES WORK: MOVING TOWARD HEALING

1. Howard Markman, Scott Stanley, and Susan Blumberg, *Fighting for Your Marriage* (San Francisco: Jossey-Bass, 1994), pp. 15-23.
2. Larry Hof, "Treating Couples—Managing Conflict: The Creative Use of Differences" (seminar of the Marriage Council of Philadelphia, 15 November 1991).
3. Markman, Stanley, Blumberg, pp. 101-104.

CHAPTER NINE: MOVING TO WIN-WIN: NEGOTIATION

1. Adapted from Larry Hof and Gerald Weeks, "Treating Couples—Managing Conflict: The Creative Use of Differences" (lecture presented at The Marriage Council of Philadelphia, 15 November 1991).

2. Howard Markman and Scott Stanley, "Negotiation," *Fighting for Your Marriage* audiotape series (Denver, Colo.: PREP, Inc., 1994).
3. Patricia Hudson and William O'Hanlon, *Rewriting Love Stories* (New York: Norton, 1991), p. 13.
4. Markman and Stanley, "Negotiation."

CHAPTER TEN: FORGIVENESS
1. For a more complete explanation on the process of intervention see Vernon Johnson, *Intervention* (Minneapolis: The Johnson Institute, 1986).

CHAPTER ELEVEN: CHANGING YOUR MARRIAGE BY CHANGING YOURSELF
1. James Dobson, *Love Must Be Tough* (Waco, Tex.: Word, 1983), pp. 44-47.
2. On self-esteem issues, we recommend Thomas Whiteman and Randy Petersen, *Becoming Your Own Best Friend* (Nashville: Nelson, 1994).

91009